故園畫憶

庚寅中秋
韓磬陸 題

《故园画忆系列》编委会

名誉主任： 韩启德

主　　任： 邵　鸿

委　　员：（按姓氏笔画为序）

万　捷	王秋桂	方李莉	叶培贵
刘魁立	况　晗	严绍璗	吴为山
范贻光	范　芳	孟　白	邵　鸿
岳庆平	郑培凯	唐晓峰	曹兵武

故园画忆系列
Memory of the Old
Home in Sketches

邢台太行古村落
The Ancient Xingtai Villages of Taihang Mountain

韩秀强　绘画
李振旭　张军昱　撰文
Sketches by Han Xiuqiang
Notes by Li Zhenxu & Zhang Junyu

学苑出版社
Academy Press

图书在版编目（CIP）数据

邢台太行古村落 / 韩秀强绘画；李振旭、张军昱撰文. — 北京：学苑出版社，2019.1
（故园画忆系列）
ISBN 978-7-5077-5646-3

Ⅰ. ①邢… Ⅱ. ①韩…②李…③张… Ⅲ. ①村落—介绍—邢台 Ⅳ. ①K922.25

中国版本图书馆CIP数据核字（2019）第004180号

责任编辑：任彦霞
出版发行：学苑出版社
社　　址：北京市丰台区南方庄2号院1号楼
邮政编码：100079
网　　址：www.book001.com
电子信箱：xueyuanpress@163.com
联系电话：010-67601101（营销部）、67603091（总编室）
印　刷　厂：北京赛文印刷有限公司
开本尺寸：889×1194　1/24
印　　张：7
字　　数：206千字
图　　幅：120幅
版　　次：2019年2月第1版
印　　次：2019年2月第1次印刷
定　　价：68.00元

目 录

序　　　　　　　　　　　　　　　　李振旭

英谈村

东寨门	3
西寨门	4
南寨门	5
北寨门	6
石楼群	7
街巷和民居（一、二）	8~9
石桥	10
贵和堂主楼	11
贵和堂主院落	12

鱼林沟村

李家庄石楼群	15
李家庄民居（一至五）	16~20
李家庄街巷和排水道（一、二）	21~22
李家庄门楼（一、二）	23~24
杨家庄民居（一至四）	25~28
杨家庄石拱桥	29
朱家庄民居	30
朱家庄民居大门	31
郭家庄石楼群	32
郭家庄民居	33
郭家庄"断壁"石楼	34

郭家庄东沟石桥	35
房顶	36
门锁	37
石梯子	38
石井与石臼	39
石磨	40
柿子削皮器	41
挎篮	42
木背架	43
排子车箱	44

茶旧沟村

村门	47
民居建筑群	48
石楼	49
民居（一、二）	50~51
宋玉庭故居（一至三）	52~54
排水系统	55
储物台	56
门楼	57
门檐	58
窗户	59
石碾子和瓷瓮	60

龙化村

皋门	63
民居（一至三）	64~66
屋顶	67
花墙	68
影壁	69
门楼	70
门洞（一、二）	71~72

崔路村

内宅	75
门楼（一至五）	76~80
门洞（一、二）	81~82
厢房（一、二）	83~84

王硇村

街巷（一至三）	87~89
民居（一至三）	90~92
碉楼	93
院落	94
碾棚	95
驴槽	96

绿水池村

阁门	99
民居（一至三）	100~101
柴草房	103
影壁和门楼	104
屋顶和石墙	105

门洞	106
古井	107
峡沟水库	108

三王村

民居（一至三）	111~113
院落（一至四）	114~117
门楼	118
门楼炉口砖雕	119
药王庙	120

神头村

民居（一、二）	123~124
门楼	125
厦棚	126
扁鹊庙（一至三）	127~129
神头庙会	130

黄岔村

雪景	133
民居（一、二）	134~135
门洞	136
石桥	137
石台阶和石碾子	138
汉阙（一、二）	139~140

后记	141
鱼林沟村全景图、茶旧沟村全景图	145~148

Contents

Preface   Li Zhenxu

Yingtan Village

East village gate	3
West village gate	4
South village gate	5
North village gate	6
The stone buildings	7
Streets and buildings (1)~(2)	8~9
The stone bridge	10
The main building of Guihe Hall	11
The main courtyard of the Guihe Hall	12

Yulingou Village

Stone building group of Lijiazhuang	15
The houses of Lijiazhuang (1)~(5)	16~20
Drainage channels in Lijiazhuang (1)~(2)	21~22
The gatehouse (1)~(2)	23~24
Yangjiazhuang houses (1)~(4)	25~28
Yangjiahzuang stone arch bridge	29
Zhujiazhuang houses	30
The gate of Zhujiazhuang houses	31
Guojiazhuang architectural complex	32
Guojiazhuang house	33
Broken building of Guojiazhuang	34

Donggou stone bridge	35
The roof	36
Door lock	37
Stone ladder	38
Stone well and stone mortar	39
stone mill	40
Persimmon peeler	41
Baskets	42
Wooden back frame	43
Caravan box	44

Chajiugou Village

The door of the village	47
The architectural complex of houses	48
Stone buildings	49
The houses (1)~(2)	50~51
Former residence of Song Yuting (1)~()	52~54
Drainage system	55
Storage platform	56
The gatehouse	57
Door eave	58
Window	59
Stone mill and porcelain urns	60

Longhua Village

Gaomen gate	63
Houses (1)~(3)	64~66
The roof	67
Flower wall	68
Folk house's screen wall	69
The gatehouse	70
Doorway (1)~(2)	71~72

Cuilu Village

Main building of Liu family courtyard	75
The gatehouse (1)~(5)	76~80
Doorway (1)~(2)	81~82
The wing room (1)~(2)	83~84

Wangnao Village

Streets and lanes (1)~(3)	87~89
Houses (1)~(3)	90~92
Residential towers building	93
The courtyard	94
Grinding shed	95
Troughs for Donkeys	96

Lvshuichi Village

Pavilion gate	99
Houses (1)~(3)	100~102
Firewood house	103
Residential shadow wall and gatehouse	104
The roof and the walls of houses	105
The doorway	106

Ancient well	107
Gorge Reservoir	108

Sanwang Village

Houses (1)~(3)	111~113
Interior of main residential courtyard (1)~(4)	114~117
Gatehouse	118
The head wall engraving of the gatehouse	119
Yaowang Temple	120

Shentou Village

Exterior view of ordinary residential building (1)~(2)	123~124
Gatehouse	125
The shed	126
The panorama of Bian Que Temple (1)~(3)	127~129
The Shentou Temple Fair	130

Huangcha Village

Huangcha in snow	133
Houses (1)~(2)	134~135
Doorways of ordinary families	136
Stone bridge	137
The stone steps and stone mill	138
Han Palace (1)~(2)	139~140

Postscript

Postscript	143

The panorama of Yulingou Village & The panorama of Chajiugou Village	145~148

序

  历史学家考证，邢台先民善于掘井，故远古时期邢台被称为"井方"，"井人"筑城即为"邢"。西周初年，邢侯筑台祭天，"邢侯台"成为一方名胜。基于此，北宋宣和二年（1120年）此地首次被称为"邢台"。在邢台市达活泉公园东南考古出土的战国时期的陶器上，"䵮"（邢）字的左边分上下两部分，上部是"井"，下部是"土"；右边是"邑"。此可证明"邢"地是一个有水可饮用、有田可耕种的都邑，是一个宜居宜业之地。

  邢台背靠高大险峻的太行山脉，面向川流不息的古黄河，大沙河、七里河、小黄河、牛尾河、白马河、小马河、李阳河、泜河等多条河流自西向东汇流于此。山前台地广袤，河流冲积扇土质丰饶，加上雨热同期的气候，邢台成为"依山凭险、地腴民丰"之地，从而有了"五朝古都、十朝雄郡"的辉煌历史。

  邢台作为不同朝代的级别不同的政治、经济、文化中心，周边历史悠久的古老村落甚多。自20世纪50年代开始在邢台一带进行的一系列考古发掘工作，证明情况确实如此。

  由于农村社会剧烈变革以及建筑材料变化、自然灾害尤其是水灾等原因，现存古村落多建于明清时期，分布于京广铁路以西的太行山区及其丘陵地带。其古村落充分体现了天人合一思想，选址顺应自然、趋利避害；街巷院落布局依循山水脉络，尽量少占耕地。目前，这些古村落中，既保存着古老而富有地方特色的民居，又遗留有寺庙、道观、石碑、戏楼、寨墙、商路、井、桥、生产生活用具等物质文化遗产，并继续演绎着悠久而多彩的民间传统习俗。可以说，邢台太行古村落，历史悠久、文化厚重，是北方农耕文明的活化石，有很高的历史文化和保护利用价值。

  正是基于上述认识，自2009年以来，我们一直致力于邢台一带太行古村落的考察和研究，先后考察了80余个保存较为完好的古村落。除了积极呼吁各界保护外，还以各种方式传播古村落文化。为此，我们尝试用钢笔写实手法和文字说明相结合的方式，绘制和编写了这本《邢台太行古村落》，希望为这些古村落得到很好的保护和良性发展做出一些努力。

本书中，在古村落的选择上，我们兼顾村落的典型性和地域分布的均衡性，主要展示太行山区邢台县、沙河市、内丘县境内的古村落。对每一个古村落，简单介绍其概况、民居建筑、民俗风情和历史传说，并努力展示其活态的生产生活方式，例如，对门墩、石桥、石井、石碾、石臼、挎篮等多有表现。同时，注重梳理村落的优良民风民俗以及红色历史。

由于水平有限，不足之处请读者批评指正。

李振旭

2018年10月20日

Preface

Historians have verified that the first inhabitants of Xingtai were adept at digging wells. Accordingly, before the Zhou Dynasty, (during ancient times) Xingtai was originally called the "Well Place". (The "Well" people built the city called "Xing". In the early years of Xizhou, Xing officials built platform to worship god, "Xinghoutai" became a place of interest. Owing to this, this place was first called "Xingtai" in 1120.) On pottery unearthed in Xingtai City's Dahuoquan Park dating back to the Warring States Period, the left side of the character "xing" was divided into two parts, with the character "well" on the top, "earth" at the bottom, and "city" on the right. This suggests that the land of "Xing" was a city of drinkable water and cultivatable fields, and it was a suitable place to live in and work at.

Indeed, the geographical environment surrounding the ancient Xingtai villages resembles this description. These villages rest against the towering Taihang Mountains, facing the ancient Yellow River. The source of many rivers such as the Dasha, Qili, Xiaohuang, Niuwei, Baima, Xiaoma, Liyang and Zhi Rivers, originate in the Taihang Mountains, where they begin their eastbound journey. With mountains and expansive, fertile riverside soil, in addition to seasons that feature heat and rain in the same period, Xingtai has always been a prosperous land with a glorious history. It used to be "capitals for five times, shrines for ten times".

As an economic, political and cultural center, many villages have naturally clustered around Xingtai. Since the beginning of the 1950s, after a series of archaeological excavations, further archaeological findings suggest the historical prominence of the region.

Due to changing construction materials, natural disasters—especially floods—and other drastic changes occurring in the rural countryside, the currently existing villages of Xingtai were formed in the Ming or Qing Dynasties, distributed along the hilly areas surrounding the Taihang Mountains, west of the Beijing-Guangzhou Railway. Village layout conforms to natural surroundings, using the terrain to maximize advantages and minimize disadvantages; furthermore, streets and alleys follow the contour of nearby mountains and rivers, while occupying as little land as possible, reflecting unity between nature and man.

Not only did the ancient Xingtai villages of Taihang preserve local historical folk houses, but they also maintained material artifacts and passed along other cultural heritages such as Taoist temples, stone tablets, theater stages, bulwarks, commercial roads, wells, bridges, tools used in daily life, and so on. These villages moreover have continued to serve as storehouses for age-old, colorful folk customs. It could be said that the mountainous Taihang area and its surrounding villages have a long history and rich culture, transmitting relatively consistent cultural traditions. The area functions as a well-preserved living fossil of northern farming civilization. It is thus a precious gift left by our ancestors.

Based on these understandings, since 2009, we have been devoted to the investigation and research of ancient Xingtai villages. We have discovered more than 80 well-preserved ancient Taihang villages and are actively calling for the protection and cultural transmission of these ancient villages. To this end, we have attempted through realism and description to compose this book. We hope that the ancient villages of Xingtai can be well protected, utilized and developed.

In the process of selecting which villages to profile, we attempted to balance a village's classical representativeness and its geographical placement. We sought to highlight the ancient villages within Taihang Mountains' Xingtai County, Shahe City and Neiqiu Country. For all selected villages, we offered brief introductions on their general situations, the architecture of their folk houses, folk customs, and historical legends. We strove to show the active state of their production lifestyle, in choosing examples like gate blocks, stone bridges, stone wells, stone mills, stone mortars, baskets and so on for depiction in this book..

At the same time, we also paid attention to organizing and presenting the villages' resplendent folk customs as well as their red histories.

Due to our limited knowledge, mistakes are inevitable. I sincerely hope readers will forgive and correct us where they occur.

Li Zhenxu
Oct 20, 2018

英谈村
Yingtan Village

英谈村位于太行山深处，距邢台市70千米，属邢台县路罗镇管辖，全村有约240户人家，670多口人。相传该村原是唐代末年黄巢起义军留下的营盘，岁月流逝，发音以讹传讹，"营盘"逐渐演化为英谈。明永乐年间，山西路姓举家迁来落户后，得以规模发展。

　　英谈村的大多数村民姓路，有一姓三支四堂之说。路姓人有三支，三支又分设德和堂、汝霖堂、贵和堂、中和堂四堂。三支四堂鼎盛时，其土地遍及冀晋豫交界处五县，商号遍布晋冀鲁豫和京津等地。

　　英谈村现存古建筑多为明清遗存，67处红石院落依山就势、高低错落。每个院落都留有后门，院院相通，既方便村民和谐相处，又便于疏散和逃生。当地人笑谈，端着碗吃饭可以串遍各家各户。村内有36座石孔桥，还有古石栏杆、龟背石影壁、古井、一滴泉等古迹。漫步村中，随处可见石臼、石杵、石磨、石碾等原生态生活用具，英谈人仍然用它们捣豆沫、磨豆腐、碾米磨面、拐米浆、摊煎饼，享受着原生态的生活美味。

　　不信鬼神敬堂口，是英谈村与其他山村迥然相异的独特风俗。在这里是看不到土地神和山神等各种神龛和神庙的，这极有可能与路姓四堂叱咤风云的商业史以及他们为富且仁的处世方式有关。目前，村民们对坐落在村中央的四大堂口依然满怀崇敬，逢年过节都要到自己所属的堂口去献香祭祖，红白喜事也要由堂口主持人帮助操办，家庭纠纷由堂口主持人调解。

　　英谈，一个山清水秀的太行古堡，一个人文荟萃、充满商史传奇的石寨，敞开怀抱等着你的到来。

Yingtan Village is located deep in the Taihang Mountains, 70km away from Xingtai City. Administratively, it is under the jurisdiction of Luluo Town, Xingtai county. The village has 240 households, totaling over 670 residents. It is said that the village was originally a military camp leftover by the Huangchao insurrectionary army in the late Tang Dynasty. With the passage of time, the name of the camp slowly transformed from "Yingpan" to "Yingtan". During the Yongle Period of the Ming Dynasty, the Lu family moved from Shanxi to Yingtan to settle and large-scale development began.

There is a saying in Yingtan that a surname must have three branches and four halls. Most villagers' last name is Lu. Lu has three branches, and three branches are divided into four halls. The four halls refer to Dehe Hall, Rulin Hall, Guihe Hall, and Zhonghe Hall. At the height of prosperity, they belonged to the richest people. Their land covered five counties at the junction of Hebei, Shanxi and Henan province. Their trades spread across Shanxi, Hebei, Shandong, Henan, Beijing and Tianjin Provinces.

Most of the existing buildings are remains from the Ming and Qing Dynasties. 67 red stone courtyards are located on the mountain at various elevations, in classic Ming and Qing Dynasties architectural style. The courtyard of Yingtan has a back door. Each courtyard is connected. When natives chat and eat with bowls in their hands, they freely walk between different family grounds. This not only facilitates the harmonious coexistence of villagers, but also facilitates evacuation and escape in case of emergency. There are 36 stone bridges in the village, ancient stone balustrades, a stone wall with carved murals containing a turtle shell, ancient wells, poetic spring and other historical sites. Wandering in the village, stone mortars, stone pestle, buhrimill, stone mill and other original subsistence tools can be seen everywhere. Yingtan people still use them to pound bean froth, grind tofu, rice, grains, pound rice pulp and make pancakes. Locals enjoy the beauty of the simple life.

Crossing into each of Yingtan's courtyards, there are no shrines or temples to the gods of the land and the gods of the mountains, making them very different from other villages. This is one of the traditional customs of the village. They do not worship ghosts and gods but instead worship at ancestral temples. This is likely to be related with the legendary business history of Lu's four halls, and their rich and humanitarian behavior. The villagers are full of reverence for the four great halls located in the center of the village. They offer sacrifices to their ancestors during festivals. Wedding and funeral are presided over by the presenter of the hall; moreover, family disputes are mediated by him.

Yingtan, an ancient fortress featuring beautiful scenery, an excellent environment and typical Taihang architectural style, thus represents a gathering of humanity and red stone constructions, replete with legends of commerce and glorious historical tales. Yingtan is waiting for you.

东寨门

英谈村的寨墙和四门,修建于清咸丰七年(1857年)九月。寨墙随地形而建,依山坡蜿蜒起伏,宽三米;高低不等,最高达六米。东寨门的下部由红石垒砌,其阁楼则用青石块建成。阁楼的梁架上绘有云纹、花卉等图案,朴实大方。

East village gate

The walls surrounding Yingtan and its four gates were built in september of the seventh year of Xianfeng in the Qing Dynasty. The walls were built in conjunction with the topography. They rise and fall along with the terrain. They are 3 meters wide and differ in height, rising as high as 6 meters in some places. The lower wall of the east gate was built with red stone, and the upper was built with blue stone. The loft's beams were painted with images of clouds, flowers and other patterns. The decoration is plain and natural.

> 西寨门

　　英谈村西寨门的墙体主要是红石块，上部间有少许青石块。西寨门外有一条上坡路，走进寨门就能看到层层叠叠的古石楼。

West village gate

This picture displays the scene near the west gate of Yingtan. The lower and upper parts of the wall are mainly composed of red stone, and the upper part is also interspersed with blue stone. An uphill road is outside the west village gate. When you enter through the gate, you can see the layers of the ancient stone buildings.

南寨门

南寨门的墙体为青石垒砌,红石块裹圈。一棵老槐树对着寨门,孤独地站立在石岗之上,其外侧河谷里有一条清澈见底的溪水。老树溪流一起伴随代代英谈人享受着太行深山的清风明月。图为英谈村南寨门外的景象。

South village gate

The walls of the southern village gate are made of blue stones and encased in red stone. An old pagoda tree stands alone on the stone hillock opposite the gate of the village. In the southern river valley, the stream is gurgling. The old tree and stream are accompanied by generations of Yingtan villagers under the clear wind and bright moon deep in the Taihang Mountains. This picture shows the scene near the south gate.

北寨门

图为英谈村北寨门外景。北寨门用红石垒砌而成。出寨门下坡是山沟，山沟里长满了核桃树、栗子树。

North village gate

This picture captures the scene outside the north gate of Yingtan. The north gate was made of red stone, and the downhill slope outside the gate leads to a ravine. Walnut and chestnut trees line the hillsides.

石楼群

  图为自英谈村东寨门进村后,站在村小学门口小广场上看到的情景,层层叠叠的石头民居随坡就势、错落有致。英谈村的石楼绝大部分两三层高,用当地盛产的红石筑成,条石砌墙,石板覆顶,远看如石筑城堡。

The stone buildings

This picture features Yingtan's stone buildings as seen from the small square at the entrance of the village primary school after entering the village through the east gate. Yingtan's old buildings were mainly constructed with the red stone that abounds in the local area. The wall was built with boulder strip. Square stones cover the top. Most stone residences feature a layered construction plan. Most of the buildings are approximately two or three stories high, built alongside the mountain, leaning against and scattered across the slope.

街巷和民居（一）

图为英谈村的某处街巷和民居。英谈村的街巷大多由石板铺就，曲曲折折。民居石楼上下层的窗户一般为上圆下方，窗花有海棠、制钱、元宝、如意、龟背等形状，寄寓了英谈人对美好生活的期盼。

Streets and buildings (1)

This picture depicts the streets and residences of Yingtan. The stone streets zig and zag throughout the village. Upper windows are generally rounded, and lower windows are generally squared. The window-cuttings are in the shapes of begonia, money, Chinese ingot, jade, tortoise back and so on. The window shape reveals expectations local Yingtan people hold for what constitutes a good life.

街巷和民居（二）

图为英谈村的另一处街巷和古民居。英谈古民居大多集中在村庄的西北部，建于明代和清代早期。所用石块比较小，也不甚整齐。这分明是人力物力有限造成的。

Streets and buildings (2)

This picture shows the early houses of Yingtan. Most of the early houses in Yingtan Village were located in the northwestern part of the ancient village enclosed within its walls. Built in the early Ming and Qing Dynasties, the stones used were small and not arranged in an orderly fashion, which was obviously a factor of limited human and material resources.

石桥

英谈村依山而建,溪流从村中流过,石桥就成为不可或缺的交通设施。全村共有大小石桥36座,均为单孔红石桥。图为英谈村西寨门里侧的景象。

The stone bridge

The stone bridge is built over the stream that flows through the village, and it has become an indispensable facilitator of traffic. There are 36 stone bridges in Yingtan Village, all of which are single-bore red stone bridges. The picture reveals the scene near the stone bridge inside the west village gate.

{贵和堂主楼}

图为英谈村贵和堂主石楼的东半部分。贵和堂主楼是两层石楼，一层明柱挑梁，六根笔直的木柱支撑厦檐，厦檐下有11个装饰性木枋。二层为三明两暗结构。宽门大窗，窗花雕刻精美，有田字套、海棠、铜钱、元宝和万字不到头等形状。

The main building of Guihe Hall

The picture shows the eastern half of the main stone building in the village. The main building of Guihe Hall is a double-layered stone structure, with one floor of open pillars on which 6 erect wooden pillars support the building's eaves, with 11 decorative timber beams underneath the structure. The second floor is arranged to feature "three light and two dark", with a wide door and large window. The window-cutting is exquisite.

贵和堂主院落

图为英谈村贵和堂主院落西北角景象。配房屋顶石板向前突出，起到为门窗遮阳避雨的作用。二楼窗户上圆下方，犹如粮囤。一层窗户现已换成玻璃窗。

The main courtyard of the Guihe Hall

The picture shows the northwest corner of the main courtyard of the hall. The roof tiles of the matching room are protruding forward, acting as a window shade and rain buffer. Second floor windows on the circle below, as if supplies, u layer of windows have been replaced by occidental glass windows.

鱼林沟村

Yulingou Village

鱼林沟村地处太行山深山区，距邢台市区53千米，属邢台县路罗镇管辖。鱼林沟村北靠青羊、黑犬双垴，左有青龙岭，右为百虎山，南朝笔架、马鞍山，处于群山环抱、三溪汇合之处，依山傍水，风景秀丽，因此吸引了不同姓氏的先民相继迁来此地定居。该村现有人口350户，1200余人。

据沟口石碑记载，村庄建于清朝初年，最初不同姓氏的长辈就村名问题进行磋商，为了体现村民平等，决定不以姓氏而是根据村中溪流有三块鱼鳞状石头来命名——村民认为这是神灵的昭示，象征着生活的富足和充裕，就把村名定为鱼鳞沟。20世纪70年代鱼鳞沟演变为鱼林沟。

鱼林沟村的居民以姓氏聚居，形成了村民们俗称的李家庄、杨家庄、朱家庄、郭家庄等自然聚落。鱼林沟村主体分布于鱼林沟西沟和东沟交汇地带，民居随山就势、因地定形而建，石楼错落有致、层次分明，院落布局合理。全村共有青石、红石建筑600余座，4000多间，近3万平方米。古民居多为明清石木结构建筑，其中，李家庄的信义堂、德昇堂等院落建筑质量上乘，建筑规模较大，保存完好。因为地处深山沟谷地带，鱼林沟村内有不少石桥，并沿街巷修建了良好的地下排水设施。

1940年，八路军太行行署六专署曾在鱼林沟村的山坡上兴建毛纺厂。国民党河北省政府主席鹿钟麟曾在该村李家庄居住，李家庄至今遗留其躲避日机轰炸的防空洞。郭家庄仍保留有被日本侵略者烧毁石楼的残垣断壁。

美丽的神话传说、规模可观的太行古石楼、可歌可泣的抗日历史，为鱼林沟村增添了几分浓浓的文化底蕴。

Located deep in the Taihang Mountains, Yulingou Village is 53 km away from the Xingtai urban area and 3 km west of Luluo Town. Luluo Town has jurisdiction over this village. North of Yulingou Village are two little hilltops named Qingyang and Black Dog. On one side is Azure Dragon Ling, on the other is Baihu Mountain, and the south is surrounded by mountains like Penholder and Ma'an Mountains. It is shady under the trees there; three streams also converge nearby, and their gurgling melody has attracted untold generations of ancestors to settle in the surrounding area. The village now has a population of 350 households and more than 1200 residents.

According to the stone stele at the entrance of the ditch, the first wave of different-named settles held meetings on the issue of naming the village names. In order to stay neutral and not privilege one family's surname over the other, the elders decided not to call the village by surname, but rather gave it a name based on the fact that there were three fish-scale stones in the stream that passed through the village. The villagers believed that these stones symbolize abundance and were a sign of divine origin.

Accordingly the village was originally named after the fish-scale stones, and then later the name changed to Yulingou in the 1970s.

Families surnamed Li, Yang, Zhu, Guo, and so on are settled in Yulingou Village in a distribution of residences. Because of the mountains and shape of the land, the main body of the village is distributed around the intersection of Xigou and Donggou. The courtyards are proportionally spaced, the stone floor is pristine, and the overall village layout is rational and sensible. The ancient buildings of Yulingou Village are built mostly with stones and wood in the style typical of the Ming and Qing Dynasties. The village has over 600 blue stone and red stone buildings, totaling over 4000 rooms and nearly 30000 square meters. Among them, Xinyi Hall, Desheng Hall and other courtyards in Lijiazhuang are of high quality, large in scale and well preserved. Because it is located deep in the mountains and valleys, many stone bridges are necessary in Yulingou Village, and sturdy underground drainage canals have been built along the streets and lanes.

In 1940, the Sixth Taihang Department of the Eighth Route Army built a wool-spinning factory in Yulingou Village. Lu Zhonglin, Chairman of the Kuomintang Hebei Provincial Government, once lived in the village of Lijiazhuang. Guojiazhuang still remains, despite portions being burned down by Japanese aggressors.

Replete with beautiful and moving myths and legends, the distinctive and towering Taihang Stone Tower as a symbol of historic resistance in the War of Resistance against Japan enhances the strong cultural background of Yulingou Village.

李家庄石楼群

在鱼林沟村，百年以上的石头房墙体主要以青砂岩石垒砌，百年以内的民居建筑墙体青砂岩石与红砂岩石兼而用之。鱼林沟石头房的 85% 为二层楼房，二层楼高六七米，三层楼高九至十米。图为李家庄石楼群。

Stone building group of Lijiazhuang

In Yulingou Village, more than one-hundred-year-old stone house walls have been mainly composed of blue sandstones. Less than one-hundred-year-old building walls were made of both blue sandstones and red sandstones. Eighty-five percent of the stone houses in Yulin Valley are two-story buildings, with the second floor reaching roughly six or seven meters high and the third floor approximately nine to ten meters. This picture shows the group of stone buildings that make up Lijiazhuang.

李家庄民居（一）

图为李家庄的一处普通民居。主楼、配楼、杂物院的石头平房高低错落。山墙顶部有三角形通风口，是用三块石板相互依靠支撑起来的。这种设计虽然简单，却功用不凡。图中的小石桥，是主街通向鱼林沟河对岸几个院落的必经通道。

The houses of Lijiazhuang (1)

This picture shows an ordinary residential area in Lijiazhuang. The stone bungalows of the main building, auxiliary buildings and multi-purpose yard are scattered at random. Three stone slabs are used to support two right-angle triangular vents on the top of the head wall. The design is simple, but the function is extraordinarily effective. The small stone bridge in the picture is the only passageway, leading from the main street to several courtyards across the Yulingou River.

李家庄民居（二）

图为鱼林沟村李家庄信义堂东南角院落。为了防止流水冲毁门前高地而堵塞进庄道路，最初的建造者在门前土坡处垒砌了石头墙，墙的上部建有石护栏。护栏由四个方石柱和三块直立的长石板构成。石墙的下部镶嵌着两个金元宝状拴马石。护栏左侧有15级青石台阶，沿台阶可以走进院落大门。

The houses of Lijiazhuang (2)

Right in the middle of the picture is the southeast corner of the Xinyi Hall in the Lijiazhuang Courtyard. In order to prevent running water from eroding the high ground and blocking the road into the village, the original builders erected stone walls at the slope of the doorstep, with stone fences on the top of the walls. The guardrail consists of four square pillars and three upright slabs. The lower part of the stone wall is also inlaid with two golden horse-shaped stones.

李家庄民居（三）

图为鱼林沟村李家庄信义堂南面民居。邻巷石楼的窗户采用红石块裹圈，窗户上部分别雕刻"礼义仁智信"行楷大字，表明院落主人的价值追求。现在的居住者在石楼墙根搭建了储存杂物的小房子，与石楼极不协调。

The houses of Lijiazhuang (3)

Xinyi Hall can be found next to the alley into Lijiazhuang, which consists of three yards, each of which was once connected to the others. The windows of the stone building in the adjacent alleyway were rung in red stones. On the upper window is engraved "Li Yi Ren Zhi Xin" in block lettering, indicating the value pursuit of the owner of the courtyard. Today's inhabitants build small storage spaces to store miscellaneous items, incongruous with the stone structures.

李家庄民居（四）

图为鱼林沟村李家庄信义堂的西南墙角。因为不是同时期建造，并且为了突出主门楼，信义堂的西南墙角凹了进去，形成了两个90°的直弯儿，如同川西碉楼。

The houses of Lijiazhuang (4)

This picture contains the southwest corner of Xinyi Hall, Lijiazhuang, Yulingou Village. Because it was not built at the same time as other structures, and in order to assign prominence to the main gate, the southwest corner of Xinyi Hall was built concave, forming two 90-degree bends, like the Western Sichuan blockhouse.

李家庄民居（五）

　　图为鱼林沟村李家庄的德昇堂民居院落。德昇堂坐西面东是鱼林沟村单体建筑规模最大的院落。主楼高三层，长约15米，宽约5米，共有15间，220多平方米。图中右侧不起眼的小门是德昇堂门口。走进门，21级青条石台阶突兀而出，刻在第一级台阶房间上的"上山"两字告诉来客：主楼建在山上。

The houses of Lijiazhuang (5)

This picture shows the courtyard of Desheng Hall in Lijiazhuang, Yulingou Village. The small inconspicuous door on the right is the gate of the Desheng Hall. Desheng Hall is the largest single courtyard in Yulingou Village. The main building is 3 stories high, approximately 15 meters long and 5 meters wide, containing 15 rooms, totaling over 220 square meters.

| 李家庄街巷和排水道（一） |

李家庄街巷蜿蜒，青石板铺地。两旁院落的排水道与主水道相通，构成树枝状的排水网。主水道长约300米，宽一米有余，两侧用青石砌墙，顶部盖青条石或青石板，水道内高处可容人直立，矮处则要爬行。

Drainage channels in Lijiazhuang (1)

Lijiazhuang's winding streets are paved with blue stone. The ancient waterway is about 300 meters long and over 1 meter wide. The walls on either side are built with blue stone. The top of the channel is covered with blue strips of stone or blue stone. At various places along the waterway, fully grown adults can stand upright, while in other places, they must stoop and crawl. The drainage channels on both sides of the street are connected to the main waterway, forming a tree-like drainage network.

李家庄街巷和排水道（二）

　　图为李家庄排水涵洞出口附近的街巷。夏季，李家庄街巷地下排水沟的雨水由此注入村内最主要的排水沟——鱼林沟河。

Drainage channels in Lijiazhuang (2)

This picture shows a street near the exit of Lijiazhuang's drainage outlet. In the summer, rainwater from the underground drainage ditch of Lijiazhuang Street is fed into the village's main drainage ditch—the Yu Lingou River.

李家庄门楼（一）

图为李家庄信义堂的门楼。门楼双层飞檐，石板覆顶。横梁下有祥云寿星木雕，木挂落雕刻有葡萄连枝和八仙所用法器，葡萄架上雕刻仰面摘葡萄的小松鼠，意为多子多福。门楼的两个立柱耸立于九级台阶之上，垂柱有倒垂的镂空灯笼木雕，底端是石柱础，柱础下部雕刻一圈精致的莲花瓣，上部雕刻成带乳钉的石鼓，中部束腰。

The gatehouse (1)

This picture shows the gatehouse of Xinyi Hall with its double eaves and a slate roof. Wood carvings of Xiangyun Shouxing, grape twigs, and the Eight Immortals can be found under the crossbeams. These magic instruments are played with by the Eight Immortals. A squirrel carved on a vineyard picking grapes on its back, meaning "more children and more blessings".

李家庄门楼（二）

图为李家庄秀才院门楼。横梁彩绘祥云，有四个户对，中间两个雕刻为龙头形状，两边的是云朵形，下边的挂落彩绘是富有教育意义的戏剧人物，并雕刻牡丹花，门楣上阳刻两行文字，两侧的木垂柱下端雕刻成石榴灯笼形状，寓意多子多福，吉祥喜庆。

The gatehouse (2)

The picture "auspicious cloud" are painted on the crossbeam of the gatehouse of the scholar's institute. There are four pairs of crossbeams. The two in the middle are carved in the shape of a dragon head, and the other two are in the shape of clouds. Paintings hanging at their bottoms contain depictions of figures with educational meaning. Flowers and other writing have been engraved on the lintel of the door in the shape of pomegranate lanterns, which signify more offsprings more blessings and jubilation.

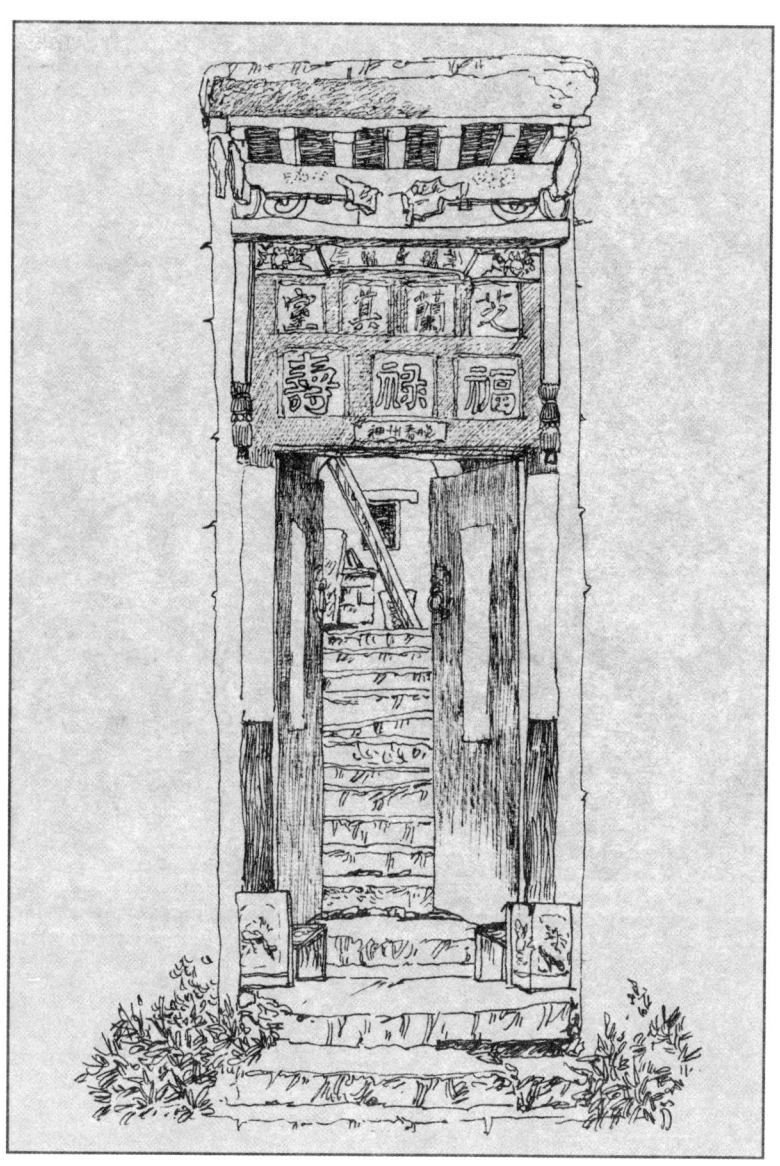

杨家庄民居（一）

杨家庄普通民居大多为二层石楼，少见精雕细刻的建筑构件，也没有繁复的窗棂。图中的木梯子在当下已经很少见。

Yangjiazhuang houses (1)

From the ancient well along the left side of Xigou upward into Yangjiazhuang, where are most of the ordinary two-story stone buildings can be found, with rare wood and stone carvings abounding, and no complicated window lattice patterns. The wooden ladder depicted in the picture is becoming increasingly rare in the countryside.

杨家庄民居（二）

  图为杨家庄临街石楼。一层门窗顶部用横直的过木支撑墙体，二层窗户用石头裹圈，上部呈圆弧形，这是鱼林沟村较为普遍的石楼门窗建筑风格。

Yangjiazhuang houses (2)

This picture shows Yangjiazhuang's streetside stone building. The topside of the first-floor doors and window is supported by a straight, wooden wall, while the second-floor window is wrapped in stone, and the upper part forms an arc. This is the common architectural style for Yulinggou's stone buildings.

杨家庄民居（三）

路边，山墙角安放着石碾，山墙上挂着电表，古老和现代并行不悖。

Yangjiazhuang houses (3)

By the roadside, there are stone mills in the corners of the head walls. The electricity meter hangs beside them, suggesting that the ancient and modern can coexist.

杨家庄民居（四）

图为杨家庄一户人家的石板屋顶。该图体现了典型的太行深山四合院落特点：空间虽小，主人仍然要在院中栽上一棵苹果树，既美化庭院，又收获果实。

Yangjiazhuang houses (4)

This picture shows the slate roof of this family, reflecting the unique characteristics of a typical courtyard in the deep mountains of Taihang: although the space is limited, the owner nonetheless planted an apple tree in the courtyard, for both aesthetic and practical purposes.

杨家庄石拱桥

  图为坐落于鱼林沟西沟上的一座石桥。石桥建于清晚期，用青砂岩石砌成，桥长 10 米，宽 3 米，高 5 米，拱圈高 3 米。

Yangjiahzuang stone arch bridge

This stone bridge is located on Xigou. The stone bridge built in the late Qing Dynasty and is made of green sandstone. It is 10 meters long, 3 meters wide, 5 meters high and the apex of the arch reaches 3 meters high.

朱家庄民居

　　图为朱家庄一户农家庭院。门旁放置石臼和水缸,成串去皮的柿子晾晒在倚靠山墙的木架子上,阶梯前的平台上摆放着几盆花草。石楼一层住人,二层放置粮食等物品。二楼山墙上开有侧窗,是为了通风,防止粮食发霉变质。

Zhujiazhuang houses

This is a farmyard in Zhujiazhuang, where the stone mortar and the water tanks are placed beside the door. Strings of peeled persimmon are drying on wooden shelves leaning against the head wall, and several pots of flowers and plants are growing on the terrace in front of the steps. People usually live on the first floor of this type of stone structure, and the second floor is generally used for the storage of grain and other goods. The second floor's side windows are opened for the purpose of ventilation, which prevents the grain from mildewing and spoiling.

[朱家庄民居大门]

图为朱家庄的一处民居院落大门。大门为铁质黑色,门楣上喷写行草大字"松竹梅",门面上部有凸起的两排乳钉和"椒图"铺首门环,中部有立体金色"福"字,做到了传统文化和现代工艺的成功结合。

The gate of Zhujiazhuang houses

This picture shows the gate of a residential courtyard in Zhujiazhuang. The gate is iron black, and its lintel is sprayed with the large characters, "Pine, bamboo and plum blossom." There are two rows of raised milk nails. The three-dimensional golden character "Fu" is in the middle of the door, successfully integrating traditional culture and modern technique.

郭家庄石楼群

　　图为站在进入郭家庄的高坡上看到的景象：石头房就地势建造，街巷和院墙并不规整。规划以节约土地、有利通行和排水为原则，做到了人与自然和谐共处。

Guojiazhuang architectural complex

This picture shows the scene on the high slope entering Guojiazhuang: stone houses were built on the terrain, streets, alleys and the courtyard walls are irregular. This suggests that planning is based on the principles of land conservation, while promoting passage and drainage. It ultimately results in the harmonious coexistence between man and nature.

郭家庄民居

图为郭家庄的一处四合院。院落的主屋是石楼,一层的门口上方建有石木结构的雨罩,二层是仓储间,有两个拱圈式窗户,另有两个门口分别通向每个厢房的屋顶,以便于晾晒和收藏农产品。这种建筑结构,在邢台西部山区富裕人家院落常见。

Guojiazhuang house

This picture shows a quadrangle courtyard in Guojiazhuang. The main house of the courtyard is on the first floor, a stone building, with a part-stone part-wood structure serving as rain cover. There is an area for storage on the second floor, featuring two arched windows, and two doorways, both of which lead to the roof of each respective room, so as to facilitate the collection and drying of agricultural products.

郭家庄"断壁"石楼

图为郭家庄一处石楼的残垣断壁。石楼左侧保存完好,右侧整体坍塌,露出了石楼内部的木架构造。此坍塌是抗日战争时日本侵略者的纵火遗迹,见证了日本"三光"政策的惨无人道。

Broken building of Guojiazhuang

The picture shows the remaining wall of a stone building in Guojiazhuang. The left side of the stone building is well preserved, but the right side collapsed, which exposed the wooden structure inside of the stone building. This was the token of Japanese aggressors during the War of Resistance against Japan, who set fire to the structure during the invasion in accordance with their the policy of "kill all, seize all, burn all".

⌈郭家庄东沟石桥⌉

　　图为郭家庄东沟石桥，位于鱼林沟东沟与西沟的汇合处。石桥是在 20 世纪 70 年代初，用青砂岩石砌成。该桥为涵洞式，一直通到对面房子后。路对面的临街石头平顶房是当时的生产队部，就坐落于涵洞桥上。

Donggou stone bridge

This picture shows Guozhuang's eastern stone bridge, located at the eastern and western junction of Yulingou. The stone bridge, was built with green sandstones in the early 1970s. On the other side of the road is a row of flat stone houses, which was the headquarters of the production team at that time.

房 顶

图为鱼林沟村的民居房顶。房顶的内部以木制三角架做支撑。在三角架上固定好檩条和椽子，上面铺盖红色或青色的石板，就构成了房顶。石板层层叠压，相互咬合，能很好地预防雨水渗漏。

The roof

This picture shows the rooftop of a residential building in Yulingou. A wooden tripod props up the interior. The purlins and rafters are fixed onto the tripod, and red or cyan slabs are layered over them. The slabs are imbricated to prevent leakage.

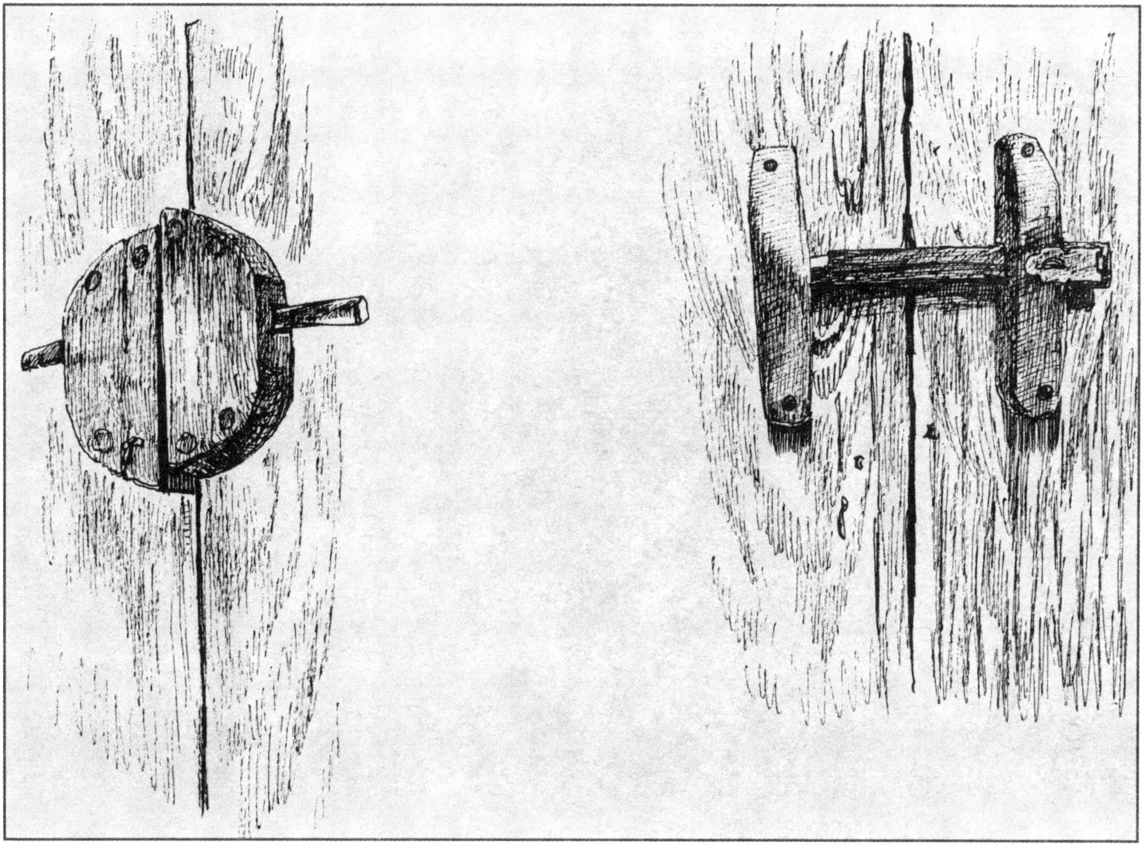

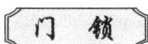

左侧图为一户人家的木制门锁，右侧图是房门里侧的木制插关。构造虽然简单，但可以封闭门户。

Door lock

On the left is a household wooden door lock, and on the right is a wooden door latch. Although the devices are simple, they allow the door to open and close.

石梯子

图为鱼林沟河中的石台阶。为防止河水泛滥，村民在河边垒砌了石墙，并选河底有硬石处，在石墙内侧垒砌几块突出墙外相互错落的青条石，作为下河的石梯子。

Stone ladder

This picture shows the stone steps near the entrance of the Yulingou River. In order to prevent the river from flooding, the villagers built stone walls on the riversides, and placed hard stones at the bottom of the river. They also set up blue strips of stones outside the prominent wall to serve as stone ladders for going down to the river.

石井与石臼

图中的石井地处村中心,据传已有 300 多年历史。井口为圆形,由一块完整的、厚约 15 厘米的大青石板凿刻而成,内径 1.5 米、外径 2 米多,历经岁月磨蚀而平滑光亮,完整无裂痕。石井附近是一个磨豆沫的石臼,目前村民仍在使用。

Stone well and stone mortar

Located in the center of the village, the well has a history spanning more than 300 years. The wellhead is round, with an inner diameter of 1.5 meters and an outer diameter of more than 2 meters, chiseled from a slab of bluestone about 15cm thick. After years of erosion, it is still smooth and bright, intact and without cracks. There is a stone mortar in use near the well. Villagers are still using it to this day.

石 磨

图为磨豆腐的小石磨。小石磨由上下两部分组成,下部的磨盘直径二尺左右,边沿凸起,在一侧留有豆浆的出口;上部的磨盘直径一尺左右,上面有一个注入豆瓣的圆孔。祖祖辈辈的鱼林沟人,就用这样的小石磨把豆瓣磨成豆浆,点上卤水就成了原汁原味的豆腐。

stone mill

This picture features a small stone mill for grinding tofu. The small stone mill is composed of two parts: the lower part is about two feet in diameter, with a bulge on its edge, and the outlet for soybean milk is on the left side; the upper part is about a foot in diameter, with a round hole on the top for injecting the beans. The ancestors of the Yulingou people used this kind of small stone mill to grind beans into soymilk, creating the original flavor of brine found in tofu.

柿子削皮器

图为柿子削皮器。该器具由上下两部分组成,下部近似于一个短板凳,上部靠右手侧捆绑一个矩形支架,支架上端右侧是把手,左手侧是三个尖形刀片。削柿子皮时,一手拿柿子,一手摇把手,把削掉皮的柿子放到下部的木凳上,再用绳子穿成一串串晾晒,就成了柿饼。

Persimmon peeler

This picture shows a persimmon peeler. The appliance consists of two parts: the lower part is similar to a short bench; and the upper part is tied to the right side of a rectangular bracket. The upper end of the bracket uses the right hand, and the left side is a three-pointed blade. When peeling persimmons, people shake the handle in one hand while taking the persimmon in the other hand. This successfully removes the skin. Afterward, the peeled persimmon is placed on the lower wooden stool, where it will be dried on a string of rope.

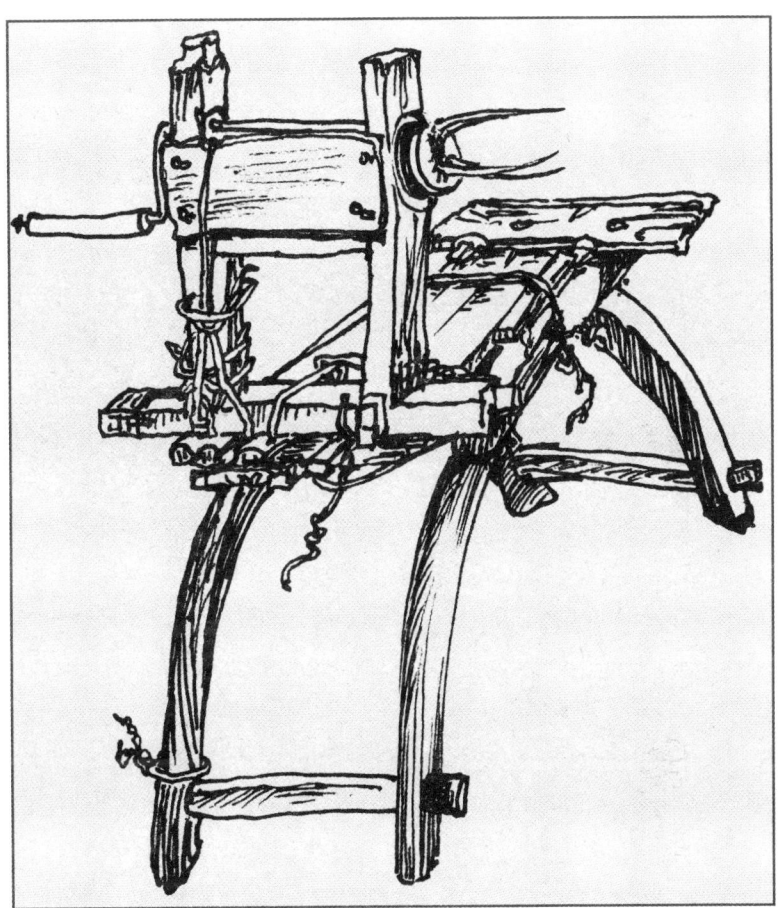

  图为两个挎篮。挎篮是用本地所生长的荆条编制而成,有圆形和椭圆形之分,直径五六十厘米,深浅不一。祖祖辈辈的太行山人,臂挎或手提挎篮,采摘果实。

Baskets

This picture shows two baskets. The baskets are made from locally grown bramble, round or oval in shape. The diameter of each bramble is approximately 50 to 60 centimeters, with varying width. Generation after generation of Taihang people carried these baskets on their arms while picking fruit.

木背架

木背架是邢台太行山区农民背柴草、干果、粮食等使用的木制工具。

Wooden back frame

The wooden back frame is a kind of wooden tool used by farmers in the Taihang Mountains area of Xingtai for carrying firewood, dried fruit, grain and so on.

排子车箱

图为排子车的车箱。排子车曾经是农村人运输货物的交通工具，上部的车箱是木架结构，下部是车轴和两个车轮。使用时，把车箱底部两侧木框上的凹槽卡在车轴上，两手拉上车辕行走。

Caravan box

This picture is the carriage of a plate-car. The plate-car used to be a means of transportation for rural people to transport goods. The upper carriage was a wooden frame structure, and the lower part had an axle connected to two wheels. When in use, stick the grooves on the wooden frames on both bottom sides of the carriage onto the axle and pull the shafts with both hands.

茶旧沟村
Chajiugou Village

茶旧沟村隶属于邢台县路罗镇，位于平涉线和邢左公路交叉点东北角的高山之巅的山坳中。村落背靠白云山，面向路罗川；四周群山环抱，树木葱茏，空气清新。股股清泉滋养村民，道道山川果硕粮丰。

关于茶旧沟村名的由来，村口石碑记载，"当时沟中有石，形如茶臼，得名茶臼沟，后写成茶旧沟"。

村落布局合理，整体和谐。站在村边山梁观望茶旧沟村，房屋大致沿等高线平行延伸，层层分布，院落依山就势建筑。青色石屋、石楼高低错落，绿树红花点缀其间，和谐自然。

民居建筑精良，精雕细刻。民居墙体以青条石垒砌，雕凿整齐，房顶石板层层叠压，滴水不漏。门墩、柱础、挂落、窗花等构件精工细作。

茶旧沟古村排水系统设计建造颇具智慧，村中主干道下建有一米多高的涵洞，院落街巷亦有流水沟槽自上而下通向主涵洞。暴雨时节，山上洪水滚滚而下，汇入地下水道，穿村而过，排入路罗川。良好的排水系统，让茶旧沟在历次水灾中安然无恙。

文脉传承，村风醇厚。行走在茶旧沟街巷，你会发现村民脸上洋溢着自信，朴实而热情好客，能随口讲出流传已久的故事。门楣上历劫余生的"耕读传家"等刻字，正是他们的为人处世之道和人生期盼，为世世代代生于斯长于斯的村民提供着精神信仰和人生导航。

茶旧沟，一个有故事的传统村落。

Chajiugou Village belongs to Luluo Town of Xingtai County, located in the depression at the top of the mountain at the intersection of Pingshe Line and Xingzuo Highway.

Regarding the origin of the village name, according to the stone table at the entrance of the village, it was thus named because "At the time, there were stones in the ditch shaped like a tea mortar, so it was accordingly called Chajiugou, which was later written as Chajiugou. The ancient village of Chajiugou is backed by Baiyun Mountain and faces Luluochuan. Surrounded by mountains, trees are lush, the air is fresh, the environment is quiet, clear springs nourish villagers, and the surrounding lands are rich in fruits and grains.

The village layout is reasonable and harmonious. Standing at the edge of the village and looking at the mountain ridge, the houses extend parallel along the ridge's contour line in layered distribution. The streets and lanes are folded and paved in accordance with the flow of rainwater, with courtyards built upon the high ground. The village blue stone houses and stone buildings have similar specifications, with green trees and red flowers interspersed between them, cohering in one harmonious and natural landscape. The three main features of the ancient village of Chajiugou are as follows.

Sturdy buildings that feature exquisite carvings. Stone carvings on the walls of residential houses are neatly chiseled, stone slabs on rooftops are made watertight by layered lamination, gate blocks, column bases, window grilles and other elaborately made. These stone buildings are basically well preserved.

Scientific design that encourages smooth drainage. The design and construction of the ancient village drainage system of Chajiugou is very smart. There are culverts more than one meter high under the main village road. Inter-courtyard lanes have top-to-bottom flow channels which drain to the main street. During heavy rain season, when the floods come down the mountainside, the village drainage system dispatches the water into Luluochuan. This excellent drainage system has kept Chajiugou safe from all previous floods.

Throughout the generations, villagers have passed along their mellow cultural mode. Walking in the streets of Chajiugou, you will find the villagers' faces brimming with self–confidence, simplicity and hospitality. They can freely tell stories that have been passed down for generations. Lintel inscriptions like "Farming, Reading, and Heritage" precisely communicate their way of life. These sort of life expectation provide spiritual beliefs and guidance for villagers born and raised Chajiugou, from generation to generation.

Chajiugou Village, a traditional village with stories.

村 门

20世纪60年代,开凿山石、砌筑拱圈、栽植柏树,形成了现在的村门。未建村门之前,人们沿着右侧的石台阶,翻过小山包,才能看到山坳中的茶旧沟。

The door of the village

In the 1960s, rocks were dug up, arches were built and cypress trees were planted, forming the present village gate. Before the gate's construction, people walked along the stone steps on the right side and climbed the hill to see the old Chajiugou Village in the mountains.

民居建筑群

图为茶旧沟村主街南口附近的景象。这里的房屋密集,有平房,有石楼,朝向不一;房顶有平顶,有坡顶;山墙形式有悬山,有硬山。无论哪种建筑样式,都是依据地势和采光需要而定。

The architectural complex of houses

Densely populated houses of bungalows and stone buildings are nearby, oriented in different directions. Roofs can be sloped or flat. Some head walls are overhanging, and some are flush. Regardless of architectural style, they are all determined byterrain and lighting needs.

石 楼

图为茶旧沟村南北主街的古石楼。茶旧沟人说,这里最初是草房。宋氏始祖于明末清初为躲避战乱和水患从邢台市西南郊大沙河北岸的羊范村迁居于此,并建房定居。后来,草房改建为了石楼。

Stone buildings

The picture shows an ancient stone building on the main street of Chajiugou Village. The people of Chajiugou say that this place was originally a thatched cottage. Song family ancestors moved here in the late Ming and early Qing Dynasties from Yangfan Village on the north bank of Dasha River in the southwest suburb of Xingtai City, escaping war and flood. Later, the cottage was converted into a stone building

民居（一）

图为茶旧沟主街南头的一处二进院落。该院落坐西面东，背靠小山梁，前后的落差很大。从前院到后院的通道是高高的石台阶，共有 27 级。

The houses (1)

The stone terrace on the west side of the south end of the main street in Chajiugou Village, along the tea road, has both an inner and outer courtyard. The courtyard rests on the east side of the western mountain ridge. The gap between the inner and outer courtyard is very large. The high stone terrace has 27 steps.

民居 (二)

主街西侧有一条南北巷子，自小巷中段西行，高高低低居住着几户人家，墙角空地上的石碾子保存完好。碾子旁的小石头房是厕所，由此可见茶旧沟人对土地的珍惜和精巧利用。

The houses (2)

There is an alley spanning north to south on the west side of the main street. Alongside it, several families live at high and low elevations, and the stone grinders on the vacant lot in the corner are well preserved and still in use. The small stone house next to the grinder is a restroom, which shows that the people in the Chajiugou understand how to effeectively use their land.

宋玉庭故居（一）

图为第一任沙河抗日县政府县长宋玉庭的故居。此院为两进院落，前院的主屋是两层石楼，一楼中央一间是二道门，门口东西两侧各有一个方正的青石门墩，分别雕刻南宋诗人范成大的《夏季田园杂兴（其七）》和宋朝大儒朱熹的《观书有感》楷体字诗句，石门墩正面里侧分别竖刻"耕传""读家"字样，横读为"耕读传家"，表明了主人的传家立世之信条。

Former residence of Song Yuting (1)

This picture shows the former residence of Song Yuting, the first governor of the Shahe Anti-Japanese County Government. The main house in the front yard is a two-story building with two doors on the first floor and two more on the second. There are square blue stone gate blocks on either sides of the front door.

宋玉庭故居（二）

图为宋玉庭故居内宅闪屏正面图景。登上11级台阶，迎面是一幅木闪屏，闪屏由两扇门合在一起而成。闪屏两侧上部是圆木柱子，下部的柱础外形上分为石墩和石柱，是一块完整的红石料做成。平时进入内宅的人需要向东西绕行，家中遇有大事和逢年过节时，才打开闪屏迎接宾朋。

Former residence of Song Yuting (2)

This picture contains the former residence of Song Yuting. When I climbed the 11 steps, I was confronted by a wooden screen made up of two doors. Log columns are on the upper sections of both screens, while the lower sections made of a complete red stone are divided into stone gate blocks and pillars. Usually, people who wish to enter the inner courtyard need to go around. When there are major events and festivals, the owners will open the flash screen to welcome guests and friends.

宋玉庭故居（三）

图为宋玉庭故居内宅闪屏背面图景。立柱上部外侧的木雕为松鼠和葡萄架，有多子多福的美好人生寓意。如今，木梁上悬挂着荆条编织的提篮，门板上挂着箅子。曾经的儒雅居所变成了普通百姓的住所。

Former residence of Song Yuting (3)

This picture features the back of the flash screen. The woodcarvings on the upper and outer sides of the column are of squirrels and vinyards, which imply more children and more blessings. Today, a basket of braided thorns hangs from a wooden beam and grates hang over the door panels. The former elegant residence has now become a scene of life for ordinary people.

排水系统

图为茶旧沟村某处街巷景象。茶旧沟村地处太行山深山区,降雨较多且集中,容易造成洪灾。茶旧沟村先人设计建造了良好的地下排水系统:主街下是完整的拱圈形排水沟,院落街巷的雨水通过大小不一的地下排水沟汇集到排水涵洞,流向村外。历经多次大洪水,茶旧沟村安然无恙。

Drainage system

Chajiugou Village is prone to floods from heavy rain. Chajiugou Village ancestors designed and built a good underground drainage system to meet this task. Under the main street is a complete arch ring drainage ditch. Rainwater from the courtyard streets and lanes collects in the main drainage culvert and pours out of village through underground drainage channels of different sizes. Despite enduring many floods, the village remains safe and sound.

储物台

在两个房屋相交形成的拐角处，村民利用几块木板和一些立柱，支撑起来形成一个不大的储物台。储物台形如吊脚楼，既方便存放家什，又充分利用了空间，可谓设计巧妙。

Storage platform

At the corner where these two houses intersect, residents have propped up several boards with columns to support them to form a small storage platform. The storage platform is shaped like a foot-hanging building, which not only facilitates the storage of household goods, but also cleverly makes full use of the space.

门 楼

图为茶旧沟村主街北头西侧一处保存较为完好的门楼。石柱础完好无损，立柱笔直，挑梁上放置两根横梁，铺设方正的木椽，石板覆顶，简洁而不失雅致。

The gatehouse

There is a well-preserved gatehouse on the west side of the main street of Chajiugou. The stone pillar foundation is intact, the vertical columns are straight, two crossbeams are placed on the overhanging beam, the wooden square rafters are laid, and the slate covers the top in a simple but elegant manner.

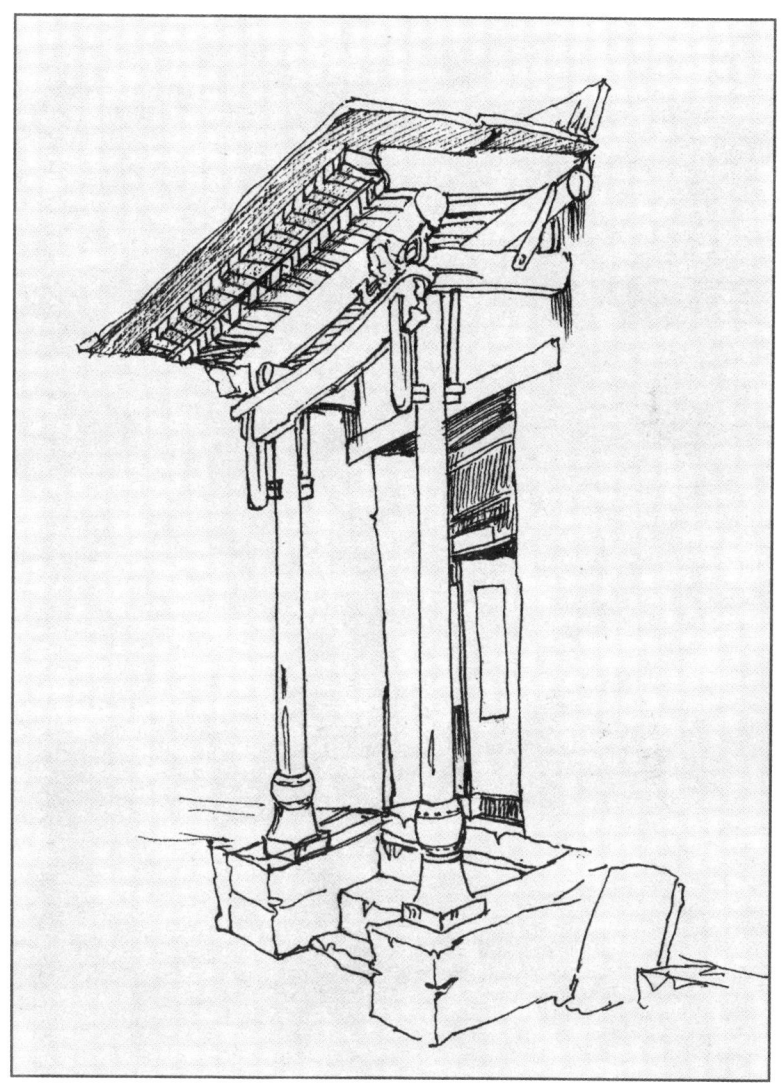

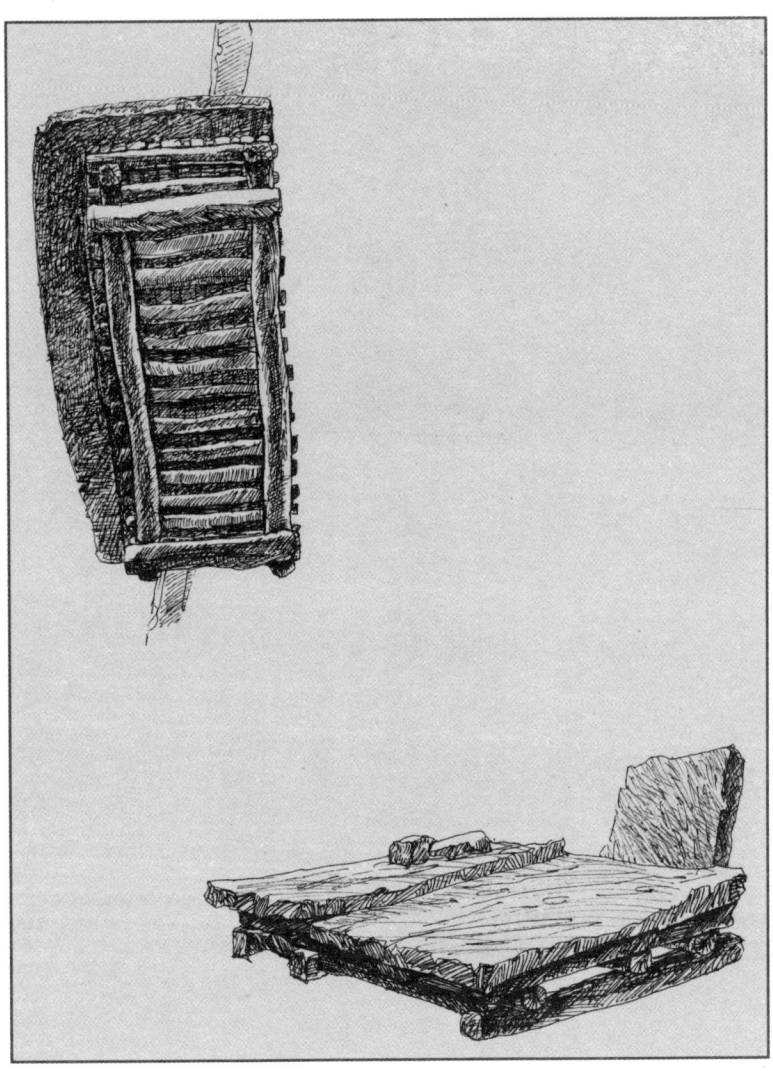

门 檐

　　茶旧沟门檐具有典型的太行建筑风格：石木结构，在挑梁上横放檩条，竖排粗壮的木椽，四角用卯榫结构固定在一起；上铺石板，坚固耐用，遮阳避雨，历经风雨而不朽。此图是门檐顶部局部图，上图是顶内面，下图是顶外面。

Door eave

The door eaves of Chajiugou have a typical Taihang architectural style, with stone and wood structures, purlines placed horizontally on the overhanging beam, strong wooden rafters arranged vertically, fixed together with mortise at the four corners. Covered with slate, it is strong and durable, providing respite from the rain and wind, immortal. This is the top of the gate, above is the inside, below is the outside.

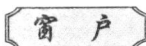 窗 户

　　图为一户人家的精致小窗，上部用精雕细刻的石块构筑成弧形圈，窗棂由田字格和中字格构成，反映了普通人家的人生期盼和处世之道。

Window

This is a household window. The upper part is composed of fine, carved stone, in an arc pattern. The lattice is composed of Chinese characters, reflecting the expectations and way of life for ordinary people.

石碾子和瓷瓮

　　茶旧沟主街路西空地上，有一盘石碾子，墙角处的石板上有三个倒置的高低不一的瓷瓮，这些都是茶旧沟人曾经的生活必需品。

Stone mill and porcelain urns

In the north, along the main street of the Chajiugou, there is a stone mill. Three upturned porcelain urns rest on the slate in the corner, which are necessities of life for the Chajiugou people.

龙化村
Longhua Village

龙化村位于邢台市西南，距离市区 22 千米，地处太行山区与丘陵区的分界线上。龙化村原名龙华底，简称龙华，20 世纪改名"龙化"。龙化村是邢台太行山丘陵地带的大村落，全村现有人口 2500 多，耕地面积 3500 余亩，村庄占地面积 4 平方千米，村域面积 24 平方千米。村西为横岭山，南北两翼有红石山峦绵延，村东有河流经过，梯田层层分布于村周边的阔谷深沟之中。

　　龙化村历史悠久。村西南一口千年古井旁有岩刻字样"武平五年（公元 575 年）四月十四日"，据此推算，龙化村已有 1400 多年的历史。据记载，明朝之前，这里有韩、程两姓人家居住。明永乐初年，范、梅、郭、张等姓陆续从山西迁来定居。明清时期，龙化村设有私塾，出过一位武进士、两位武举人、120 多名秀才，是远近闻名的文化村。

　　龙化村的街巷地面是红石板，两边是青石蓝砖房。临街有石棚，里面安装石碾、石磨供村民使用。村中古民居大多是明清或民国时期建筑，院落多为四合院，前后略长，左右对称；有五裹三或五裹四的单门独院，也有前后二进院落，院落上房均为石砖木结构的楼房。大部分民居都有雕刻精美的门楼。门楼的木挂落雕刻龙游祥云、连枝葡萄、八仙法器等图案，雕工细致、纹饰复杂、彩绘颜色厚重。木刻图案以龙居多，这在邢台太行山其他古村落民居中较为少见。

Longhua Village is located 22 kilometers southwest of Xingtai City, at the boundary between the Taihang Mountains and hilly areas. Because there is a Longhua temple on the western side of the village, and the village is under the temple, , people called it Longhua Basin, abbreviated to Longhua. In the 20th century, Longhua Village was a large village in the hilly area of the Taihang Mountains surrounding Xingtai. The village has a population of more than 2,500, with a cultivated land area over 3,500 mu. The village itself covers an area of 24 square kilometers. Hengling Mountain is to the west of the village, with red stone mountains stretching across the northern and southern wings, and rivers pass through the eastern area of the village. Terraces are distributed across the wide valley and deep gullies around the village.

Longhua Village has a long history. According to a rock-engraved inscription near the thousand-year-old village well, "April 14th, Wuping the Fifth year" refers to Longhua Village having been built at least 1400 years ago. Before the Ming Dynasty, Han and Cheng families lived here. In the early years of Yongle, Fan, Mei, Guo and Zhang households moved from Shanxi to settle in Longhua, one after another. Longhua is a well-known cultural village. During the Ming and Qing Dynasties, there were private schools in Longhua, including one martial arts scholar, two martial arts examiners and more than 120 talented people.

Many years have polished the red flagstones set in the streets and lanes. Blue bricks can be found on both sides of the streets. Occasionally, a stone mill can be seen. These mills are typically installed in the stone shed found in most buildings' first floor to facilitate convenient household use. The courtyards of Longhua Village are mostly quadrangle shaped, slightly elongated and bilaterally symmetrical; there are five single-family courtyards with three or four wrapped in five, and there are also two courtyards in the front and back. The ancient houses of Longhua were mostly built during the Ming and Qing Dynasties or during the Republic of China. Wooden hanging of carved dragon, auspicious clouds, the Eight Immortals and other patterns are carved in an exquisite, complex, and colorful array. Most wood-carved patterns here feature dragons, which is difficult to find in other villages around Xingtai..

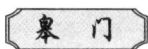

图为龙化村遗存的皋门北门洞。皋门是龙化村的东大门,原有三个门洞,南面的两个门洞已损毁。现存北门洞高 3.5 米,宽 3 米;墙体下部用青石砌成,上部为青砖白灰垒砌;顶部为木架结构,上铺沙石灰。皋门平时是村子的东大门,雨季时就成为沟通南北街道的桥梁。

Gaomen gate

This picture shows the north doorway of Gaomen gate left in Longhua Village. This structure was originally located at the east gate of the village. It had three doorways. Two doorways in the south were destroyed by flood in 1963. The lower wall of the building is made of bluestone, the upper wall is also made of blue bricks and white lime, and the top of the building is made of a wooden frame and covered with sand and limestone. The doorway is 3.5 meters high and 3 meters wide. Generally, the gate is the east gate of the village. During the rainy season, it becomes a bridge connecting the north and the south streets.

民居（一）

　　图为龙化村的一处近期民居。龙化村地处太行山丘陵区和山区结合部，三面环山，一面临水，地势不平。房子一般建在高处，进门要上台阶或坡道，这是龙化民居的特色之一。

Houses (1)

This picture shows a recently built house in Longhua Village. Longhua Village is located at the junction of the low hilly area of Taihang and the deeper surrounding mountains, with mountains on three sides and a river on another. The terrain is uneven. The house is built on the high side, and going up steps or ramps before reaching the door is characteristic of Longhua residences.

民居（二）

图为龙化村的一处典型民居。民居门前建有影壁，高台下修建洞穴以放置柴草；墙体厚近50厘米，上部是青砖，下部为青石，用白灰勾缝；临街一面的屋顶垒砌花砖墙。这是龙化村民居的特色之二。

Houses (2)

This picture depicts a typical house in Longhua Village. Carved walls with murals are built in front of the door, and a storage place is built under the porch for placing firewood. The wall is nearly 50-cm thick, and its upper part is composed of blue bricks, while its lower part is blue stone, with white-grey joints. The area of rooftop facing the street features brick flower depictions, an architectural characteristic of Longhua residential buildings.

民居（三）

　　图为龙化村一处临街带门洞的民居，俗称临街"洞房"。临街"洞房"一般为两层，一层墙体面街，并开有青石裹圈的门洞，里面安装石碾子，供街坊邻居使用；二层临街开窗，院内开门，由住户自用。

Houses (3)

Longhua Village's streetside "cave homes" are generally divided into two floors: a wall wrapped in blue stone facing the street is on the first floor, with stone mills inside for neighborhood use. The second floor features a courtyard with a window sill facing the street, which the owner can use for any purpose.

| 屋 顶 |

　　图为龙化村带有马墙的民居屋顶。龙化村古民居多四合院结构,房屋绝大多数是平顶。屋顶为白石灰和砂石混合捶打而成。

The roof
Longhua Village dwelling rooftops are typically quadrangular, with flat roofs made from a mixture of limestone and sand.

花 墙

图为龙化村民居的花墙。屋顶上的花墙用青砖青瓦垒砌而成,巧妙支撑的青瓦构成铜钱和海棠花图案——吹来的风能够顺利通过,可增强花墙的牢固性,同时寓意堂中有钱、家财万贯,既具建筑美感,又兼具功能性。

Flower wall

This picture features houses with flower walls in Longhua Village. The wall on the roof is made of blue bricks and tiles. The skillfully supported tiles form patterns of copper cash and begonia flower. The wind can pass through the passageway smoothly. This type of design not only has profound architectural the aesthetic sense but also reflects the residents' life expectations, while increasing the structural integrity of the wall.

影壁

图为龙化村一处民居前的影壁。该民居建于高台之上，为避免大门正对道路或水坑、池塘，就在门外高台上建筑影壁。进门台阶修建于影壁旁。

Folk house's screen wall

This picture is a wall with mural carvings in front of a residence. Because the house is built on a high platform, there is a terrace space in front of the door. The screen wall is built on the terrace opposite the door. Stone steps are built beside the screen wall to prevent the door from directly facing either a water hole or the road.

门 楼

图为龙化村某民居的门楼。门楼横梁下装饰龙首翼拱和鲤鱼荷花木雕；木挂落上半部分阳刻八仙和吉祥结，下半部分镂空和阳刻结合，雕刻了两对狮子戏铜钱；木垂柱阳刻祥云暗八仙，柱头为铜钱灯笼样式。两侧山墙戗檐部位各雕刻一朵海棠花和一对飞鸟；墀头砖雕硕大饱满的牡丹花，两侧饰刻草龙，上部为双狮戏绣球，下部是万字回纹。整个门楼雕刻构思奇巧，形象生动，技艺精湛。

The gatehouse

This picture shows the gatehouse of a folk house in Longhua Village. The cross beam is decorated with dragon head and carp and lotus carved in the wood arch, and the wood hanging on the upper part features carvings of the Eight Immortals. The lower section features two pairs of frolicking lions. Bronze coins are also carved onto the woodwork. The carvings are ingenious, vivid and exquisite.

门洞（一）

　　图为龙化村郭家巷子里的一个门洞。该门洞青石基座，青砖裹圈，是郭家大院内外宅的分界。门洞内是两个大院，大院门楼有精致的砖木雕刻构件，主房都是石砖木结构的楼房。门洞外右侧的院落是长工们居住的地方，墙体上雕刻精细的拴马石显示了郭家曾经的殷实和富足。

Doorway (1)

The picture shows a doorway in Guojia Lane. Bluestone is at the base of this gateway. The green brick enwraps the arch. One side is inside the Guojia courtyard, and another is outside. The gateway thus functions as a boundary. Inside the entrance are two cour tyards of the Guo family. Each of the courtyards contains exquisite brick and wood carvings, and the main rooms are made from stone bricks and wooden structures. The courtyard on the right outside of the entrance is the place where the migrant workers live. The elaborate carved stones fixed to the walls show the well-off and rich nature of the Guo family.

门洞（二）

图为龙化村郭家大院内的门洞。门洞一边通向内宅，另一边通向长工们居住的院落。如今虽然破败不堪，但其石砖结构的墙体，粗壮笔直的房顶木料仍能显示出建筑质量之上乘。

Doorway (2)
These doors lead to the main house and into the courtyard, where the migrant workers live. Though now dilapidated, its stone-brick walls, sturdy, straight roofs and timber structures still reveal a superior quality.

崔路村
Cuilu Village

崔路村位于邢左公路北侧，距邢台 15 千米，有居民 3000 余人，属邢台县南石门镇管辖。相传崔路村建于隋唐之际，因有一崔姓驿站官员管理附近道路而得名。

崔路村的民居，墙体多由石头和青砖砌成，下部为规则的青条石，上部为青砖；屋顶为木架结构，所用梁、檩和椽子都很粗壮；主房高，配房低，属典型的冀南太行山区和华北平原建房特点相结合的四合院。崔路村的各个家族都建有豪华富美的宅院，以刘家的永和堂、五世同堂、七代同居大院最具代表性。刘家大院现存有近 40 个院落，房屋 480 余间，约占全村古民居的三分之一，现大多保存完好。

崔路村古民居大门口和门楼建筑坚固，装饰精美，大气儒雅。几处大院在第二道门和第三道门都建有门楼，门楼大气精致：顶覆筒状瓦，脊站望天吼，墀头刻吉祥花卉，门头刻凝厘笃祐、备致吉祥、惠迪吉等大字。门楼墙体背面刻三多、九如等字，大字遒劲，小字清秀，图画饱满，立体感强。

崔路村现存大院是明清顺德府（今邢台市区）商业文化繁盛的真实写照，是顺德府南关经济发展的缩影，更是崔路人几百年来勤奋劳作、节俭持家的历史见证，有较高的建筑艺术和历史文化价值。

Cuilu Village is located in the north side of Xingzuo road, 15 kilometers away from the Xingtai, with a population of more than 3,000 residents. It is under the jurisdiction of Nanshimen Town, Xingtai County. According to legend, Cuilu Village was established between the Sui and the Tang Dynasties, and it was named after a post official surnamed Cui who managed the nearby roads.

The walls of the compound houses in Cuilu are made of stones and blue bricks, the lower parts regular blue strips of stones, and the upper parts blue bricks. The roofs are typically wooden frame structures with thick beams, purlin and rafters. The main house is ordinarily more prominent. Each family in the village of Cuilu has built a luxurious, rich and beautiful home, with the Liu Family Hall serving as the most typical example. Liu's Family Hall has nearly 40 courtyards and more than 480 houses, most of which are well preserved.

Cuilu's ancient residential gates and gate houses are sturdy, decorated and elegant. Brick inscriptions can be found both above the gate and on both sides of the head wall; mostly traditional or classic concise phrases,, exhorting passersby to focus on virtues such as goodness, tolerance, honesty, reading, light, benevolence, righteousness, moral integrity etc., all of which seek to encourage a pathway of growth fostered by education.

The extant great courtyard of Cuilu is an accurate portrayal of the prosperous commercial culture of the Shunde Prefecture that existed in the Ming and Qing Dynasties, a microcosm of the economic development found in Nanguan District in Shunde prefecture, as well as a historical witness of the Cuilu peoples' hundreds of years of hard work, frugality and household management, all contained in architectural high art of significant historical and cultural value.

内宅

图为崔路村刘家永和堂大院的内宅。内宅的上房一般都是两层楼，每层五间房。一层的房屋是一门两窗，门上建有一个遮阳避雨的小门檐，窗户为方形。二层房屋的窗户为上圆下方的形状，青石裹圈。屋顶是双向斜坡覆盖青瓦，脊角装饰镇宅兽。

Main building of Liu family courtyard

This picture features the inner house of the Liu family's Yonghe Hall courtyard in Cuilu Village. The inner house typically contains two floors, with five rooms on each floor, with one door and two windows on the first floor. There is a small eaves over the doorway, offering shelter from both rainfall and sunshine. The windows on the second floor have concave tops and square bottoms, and are wrapped in bluestone; the roof is a two-way slope covered with blue tiles, while ridge corners are decorated with animals.

门楼（一）

图为崔路村刘家永和堂大院的内宅门楼。崔路内宅门楼一般为双向斜坡布瓦顶，门楼上有精美的砖雕木雕构件，门头雕刻反映家风的儒家经典词句。个别门楼的背面还有木雕或砖雕的对联，时刻告诫居住者为人处世的准则。

The gatehouse (1)

The interior gatehouse of the courtyard of the Liu family is shown in the picture. The inner house is generally a two-way sloping tiled roof, while other areas of the gatehouse are covered in exquisite brick and wood carvings. Sayings from Confucian classics can be found in these carvings, reflecting family traditions, and reminding residents of the principles that govern human life.

门楼（二）

　　图为崔路村刘家七代同居大院东门内宅门楼（第三道门）正面景象。门楼为晚清建筑，砖木结构，顶部起脊扣瓦；木挂落镂空雕刻，门匾写有"惠迪吉"三个楷体大字。

The gatehouse (2)

This picture features the seven-generation residence of the Liu family (the third door). The gatehouse was built in the late Qing Dynasty out of brick and wood. The gatehouse has a ridged rooftop, featuring hanging wood and hollow carvings. Three characters are inscribed on the plague: "Hui Di Ji".

门楼（三）

图为崔路村刘家七代同居大院东门内宅门楼（第三道门）里面景象，门楼屋檐下雕刻"南极呈祥"四个行楷大字。

The gatehouse (3)

This picture reveals the interior of the third gate of the Liu family's seventh generation cohabitation courtyard in Cuilu Village. Walking away from the courtyard, when you look up, you will see the characters "Nan Ji Cheng Xiang" carved in block letters under the eaves of the gatehouse.

门楼（四）

图为崔路村刘家七代同居西院的第二道门门楼。该门楼雕工繁复而精美，木挂落雕刻连枝葡萄，山墙炉口雕刻盛开的牡丹花，寓意多子多福，花开富贵，反映了农耕社会农家人的人生期盼。

The gatehouse (4)

This picture shows the second gatehouse of the west Liu family seventh generation cohabitation courtyard. The gatehouse carvings are complex and immaculate, containing hanging trees, grapes, peony flowers in blossom etc. at the entrance of the head wall. These images signify more children and more blessings, reflecting the system of values shared by farmers.

门楼（五）

　　崔路人极其注重家风家教，不少门楼上刻有"积善余庆"、"廉忍公读"等体现优秀传统文化的词语。此图为崔路村刘家五世同堂的第二道门楼，门楼以外主要是磨坊、牲口棚、车棚等生产生活必备设施，以内分成两个院落，是全家人的居住空间。

The gatehouse (5)

Cuilu people assign tremendous importance to family traditions and education. Many gatehouse are inscribed with sayings, such as "Good deeds will be rewarded," and "honesty, tolerance, fair, reading" reflect excellent traditional cultural and literary values. Outside the gatehouse are necessary facilities, such as mills, livestock sheds, vehicle sheds, and other production and livelihood necessities. Inside the gatehouse is divided into two courtyards, which comprise the living space of the whole family.

门洞（一）

图为崔路村刘家七代同居大院东院的第二道门门洞。该门洞建于同治年间，为砖木结构，白石灰和青砖砌墙。门洞和内宅门楼之间为二进院落，有伙房、工具房和厕所。

Doorway (1)

This picture features the eastern door of the Liu family's seven generations cohabitation courtyard in Cuilu. The door was constructed in the Tongzhi period as a primarily brick and wood structure, with white limestone and blue brick masonry. The doorway and the inner gatehouse are separated by courtyards, with kitchens, tool rooms and wash rooms.

门洞（二）

　　图为崔路村赵家大院内宅门洞（第二道门）。门洞墙体由青石青砖垒砌而成。门洞式样别具一格，为正圆形，门洞上方雕刻"备致吉祥"，右侧墙体雕刻"总集福禄"，左侧墙体雕刻"凝厘笃祜"，反映了赵氏家族的修身准则和人生期盼。

Doorway (2)

This picture looks at the doorway opening of Zhao family courtyard. The wall of the house is made of bluestone and blue bricks. The doorway opening has a unique style. The carving above the door expresses "to be auspicious". The carving on the right side expresses "to gather luck". The carving on the left side is "Ning Li Du Gu". These reflect the philosophical values regarding self-cultivation and life expectations held by the Zhao family.

厢房（一）

图为崔路村刘家大院五世同堂内宅的西厢房。东西厢房均为五间，为石砖木结构，门窗都是青砖裹圈，窗格是简洁的方格。西厢房建有飞檐翘角的阁楼，是家中未出嫁的女儿们的居住之所，俗称"绣楼"。

The wing room (1)

This picture shows the west wing room and embroidery building of the Liu family courtyard. The compartments between the East and West both hold five rooms, made of stone, brick and wood. The doors and windows are blue bricks, and their panes are made of simple squares. Under the roof of the house is a loft with cornices and warped corners, where the unmarried daughters in the family dwell.

厢房（二）

　　图为崔路村刘家大院五世同堂内宅西厢房的内场景。房内有废弃不用的传统土炕，炕上放置木箱和旧家什，墙角设置通向绣楼的木楼梯。

The wing room (2)

This picture shows the west wing room. There are abandoned traditional soil kang, wooden boxes and antique household items on the kangs. A wooden staircase leading to the second floor is set in the corner.

王硇村

Wangnao Village

王硇村地处太行山东麓，为太行山余脉形成的天然屏障所环抱。全村800余人，属沙河市柴关乡管辖。村中有东西主街三条，小街10条，南北小巷13条，最长街道800余米，最长的巷道270余米。据传，明永乐年间，成都府两岗村人、武官王得才押运金银进京，途中被劫，为避免杀头之灾，王得才携一家老小辗转逃到王硇村安家落户，自此把成都一带的建筑风格带到了太行深处。

　　历经500余年建起的王硇石楼群是太行山建筑风格和成都一带建筑风格的完美结合：楼顶起脊，青瓦覆盖，飞檐翘角，五脊六兽，是明显的川寨特色；厚厚的红色石头墙则是太行山民居的符号。站在高处眺望，只见红墙黛瓦，鳞次栉比，似云若霞，蔚为大观。王硇石楼群还具备防御功能，为防止弓箭射击，街巷被设计成30~50米一拐弯的曲尺形，在街巷交叉的要道口、临街的石楼上几乎都建有碉楼，碉楼上设有瞭望孔。

　　王硇石楼多为两层或三层，现今仍处于完好状态的约130处，房屋2000余间，建筑面积7.2万多平方米，占全村现有建筑面积的百分之五十以上。

　　由于具有天然屏障，王硇成了抗日根据地名副其实的红色堡垒村，八年全面抗战中，日本侵略者一次也未能进入村中。

Wangnao Village is located at the eastern foot of the Taihang Mountains, surrounded by hills and sunken valleys, forming an expansive green backdrop of nature. There are more than 800 residents in the village, and it falls under the jurisdiction of the Chaiguan Township of Shahe City. In the village, there are 3 main streets, 10 small streets, and 13 lanes arranged on a north-south axis. The longest street spans over 800 meters, and the longest lane stretches more than 270 meters. Allegedly, during the Ming Dynasty's Yongle Period, Wang Decai, a Liang Gang villager and military officer of the Chengdu Government who escorted gold and silver to Beijing, was robbed on the road. In order to avoid being killed, Wang Decai fled to Wangnao Village with his family. Since then, the architectural style of Chengdu has been assimilated into the local Taihang area.

The Wangnao group of stone buildings, constructed over a 500-year period, reigns supreme over Taihang Mountain's architecture, as the supreme example of Chengdu's style. It contains ridged roofs covered in blue tiles, cornices with warped angles and the characteristic five ridge and six beast style obviously of Sichuan rural architecture, while on the other hand, its thick red stone walls symbolize Taihang Mountain traditional dwellings. From a high vantage point, one can observe red walls and black tiles, arranged in unending rows, like endless clouds, a feast for the eyes. This group of building also has defensive utility—streets and alleys are designed to curve, to prevent archers from having clear line of sight. These streets and alleys curve roughly every 30 to 50 meters. Moreover, all the main crossings feature towers, with lookout posts on the top.

Wangnao's typical stone buildings feature two or three floors. At present, roughly 130 buildings are still in good condition, including more than 2,000 rooms, totaling over 72,000 square meters, occupying over 50 percent of the village's total structural area.

Because of its natural barriers, Wangnao was worthy of becoming a red fort base of operations in the War of Resistance against Japan. In the eight-year-long conflict, Japanese invaders failed to penetrate the village even once.

街巷（一）

图为王硇村典型"东南缺"院落组成的巷子。巷子西侧的每个院落东厢房比主房往西，把东南部的空缺留在巷子中，前一户人家的主房与后一户人家的东厢房对齐，巷子西部自然形成错落有致的一个个直弯。这就是中国俗称的"有钱难买东南缺"。这一观念来源于"八卦"中的"巽"卦，"巽"对应东南方位，代表"风"，为顺畅、平安之意，将宅院的东南方位留出来，寓意顺畅、招财。

Streets and lanes (1)

This picture shows a typical alley found in Wangnao Village consisting of several courtyards. The main house of the former family is aligned with the east wing of the latter family, and the west side of the lane naturally forms a smooth, properly proportioned curve. This is what is commonly known in China as "Money can't buy the southeast corner." This concept comes from the "Xun" hexagram in the "Eight- Diagrams". The ancient people thought "Xun" corresponded to the southeast, also representing the wind, a symbol of both smoothness and safety.

街巷（二）

　　图为王硇村一处街巷拐角处的景象。村民为了行走便利，尤其是为了方便骡马驮运货物时通行，主动把墙角后退，垒砌为斜面或圆形，称为"拐弯抹角"。

Streets and lanes (2)

This picture is of a house on a Wangnao Village street corner. To allow for convenient walking and to facilitate efficient transportation of goods by mules and horses, villagers took the initiative to shape the corners of the walls into circles, creating roundabouts.

街巷（三）

图为王硇村的伸屈巷。由于左边人家建房早，院子向外凸出，右边人家为了保持巷子的宽度里外一致，就把自己的院墙垒砌为凹进去的弧形，由此可见王硇人的睦邻崇善之风。

Streets and lanes (3)

This picture shows a twisting lane of Wangnao Village. Because the house on the left was built earlier and the courtyard protruded outwards their own curved, the right courtyard walls were built to a concave are in order to match the width of the lane. It can be seen the good-neighborliness and goodwill of the people of Wangnao Village.

民居（一）

图为王硇村的一处明代民居。王硇村先祖初来乍到，人力财力不足，早期民居没有石楼，墙体石块较小，门面比较朴素。

Houses (1)
This picture features early Ming Dynasty folk houses of Wangnao Village. Because the ancestors of Wangnao Village were new arrivals lacking manpower and financial resources, early folk houses were not made of stone, had smaller walls and simpler facades.

民居（二）

图为王硇村的一座清代民居。古民居墙体使用当地出产的丹霞岩石垒砌，外层为较工整的条石，内层填料主要为碎石。石楼内冬暖夏凉，保温效果很好。

Houses (2)

This picture reveals a local-style Qing Dynasty-era dwelling of Wangnao Village. The walls of ancient residential buildings were built with local danxia rock, with an outer layer of neat strip stone, and inner layer of filled gravel. This type of stone structure is warm in winter and cool in summer.

民居（三）

图为王硇村沿街的一所民居。由于地处山坡，房屋依地形而建，因此街巷弯曲，村民便见缝插针地在门前垒砌羊圈和柴草间。

Houses (3)

This picture contains ordinary folk houses along one of Wangnao Village's streets. Because they are located on a hillside and must conform to the terrain, the streets and lanes are accordingly curved, and the villagers make use of all available space for building sheepfolds and firewood sheds.

{ 碉 楼 }

  图为王硇村一户人家的碉楼。碉楼下部为方形,顶部建为圆弧形,这不但契合古人天圆地方的宇宙观,还有利于排出雨水。碉楼面向街巷的墙体上设有瞭望孔。

Residential towers building

This picture shows a residential tower building in Wangnao Village. The lower section is squarelike, and the top is circular. This type of design not only conforms to the ancient notion of round sky and square earth, but is also conducive for draining rainwater.

院落

图为王硇村带有后门的一个民居院落。王硇村的老院落都开有后门，户户相通，院院相连，村内村外连通，具有防御逃生功能。

The courtyard

This picture is of a folk courtyard with a back door. The old courtyards of Wangnao Village are all interconnected through back doors. This links the outside and inside of the village, which has the added function of facilitating defense and escape.

碾 棚

　　在王砲村，碾棚一般建在街巷交叉处比较宽阔的场地，后墙挨着院落，棚口面向街巷，便于附近住户使用。棚内不但安装石碾子，还有老式风车。

Grinding shed

In Wangnao Village, grinding sheds are generally built on street corner beside wide fields, next to a back yard, with the shed opening facing the street for convenient residential use. The shed is not only equipped with stone mills, but also old-fashioned windmills.

| 驴　槽 |

图为王硇村村民养的两头毛驴及驴石槽。王硇村民有养毛驴的习惯，平常以秸秆和青草作饲料，耕作和驮运时添加黑豆和麦麸等精料。石槽用青石凿成，可以供两三只毛驴同槽食用。

Troughs for Donkeys

This picture shows two donkeys and their stone trough. They were raised by the residents of Wangnao. Wangnao Villagers have the habit of raising donkeys, using straw and grass as feed, and when they are being worked, black beans and wheat bran will be added to their meals. The stone trough is made of blue stone and can be eaten from by two or three donkeys at the same time.

绿水池村
Lvshuichi Village

绿水池村地处太行深山区，属于沙河市柴关乡管辖。该村三面环山，东向大河，村南一条季节性河流顺势而下，直通柴关。因村南龙王庙东南侧谷底青石之上有一酷似龙形的水池，故名绿水池。

　　绿水池村建于明代，现常住人口 200 多人。村民以王姓为主，分为东门王和西门王。东门王家明朝初年从山西迁移到邢台县小戈廖村，之后辗转来到绿水池落户；西门王家是明朝成都人武官王得才的后裔，王得才在王硇村安家立户，之后有一支脉来到绿水池居住。

　　绿水池村东有一座北依山坡、南近河岸的阁门。紧挨阁门是一个占地约 300 平方米的小广场，广场南侧为古戏楼，北侧为民居，西侧有一棵古槐树和带辘轳的老井。从广场西行，就进入了绿水池古村落的主街区。因为土地金贵，村内街巷较为狭窄，其中的两条主街分别叫作南股道和北股道。两条股道各自折了几个弯，通过小巷互通。南股道原来是村子的排水沟，传说是白龙居住之地，后来白龙向南滚动到村南的河谷中，腾挪出了土地，人们才在这条股道的南边建房。北股道以北地势逐渐抬高，民居随坡就势而建，小巷蜿蜒曲折而行，互联互通，便于自卫和逃生。在街巷的拐弯处，下部墙体一般凹进去，以利通行。

　　弯弯曲曲的街巷，镶砖的红石墙，片片青瓦，再加上文雅的门楼和对联，使绿水池村落既有太行山民居的古朴厚重之风，又兼有南方民居的灵秀雅致之气。

Located deep in the Taihang mountain area, Lvshuichi Village is under the jurisdiction of chaiguan Township, Shahe City. The village is surrounded by mountains on three sides and faces east toward a great river. A seasonal river south of the village runs downstream through Chaiguan. Because there is a dragon-shaped pool on the southeast side of Dragon King Temple in the south of the village, it is called Lvshuichi Village.

Lvshuichi Village was built in the Ming Dynasty. There are nearly 600 people and more than 200 permanent residents. The villagers are mainly surnamed Wang. They are divided into Wang of the Eastern Gate and the Wang of the Western Gate. In the early Ming Dynasty the Wang Family of the East Gate migrated from Shanxi to Xiaogeliao Village in Xingtai County, finally settling down in Lvshuichi. The Wangs of The West Gate are descended from Wang Decai, a military officer in Chengdu during the Ming Dynasty. Wang Decai eventually settled down in Wangnao Village, where mountains and peaks line the horizon.

Lvshuichi Village's East Gate features a pavilion gate on the south side of the mountain, near the river. Walking through the pavilion gate one immediately notices a small terrace of roughly 300 square meters. The south side of the terrace is an ancient theatre building, the north side is a residential building, and the west side is an ancient well with a windlass. West from the terrace leads into the main block of the ancient village of Lvshuichi. Because land is limited, streets and lanes in the village are relatively narrow. The two main streets are called Nangu Road and Beigu Road. The two streets have several major bends and are criss-crossed with smaller lanes. Originally, Nangu Road was the drainage ditch of the village. It is said that it was the place where the white dragon resided. Later, the white dragon rolled to the south of the village and moved out of the valley. The terrain north of Beigu Street gradually rises upward. The residential buildings there are built along this slope, with twisting alleyways. The interconnected network makes for convenient historical self-defense and escape. At the corner of most streets, the lower wall is generally concave to facilitate passage.

Winding streets and lanes, red-brick and stone walls, pieces of blue tiles, plus elegant gateways with couplets, make the village of Lvshuichi harmonize in not only its ancient mountainous style found in Taihang folk homes but also in its elegant spirit found in southern folk architecture.

$\boxed{阁\ \ 门}$

  阁门位于绿水池村村东。阁门下部的门洞是村里的排水通道，用青石垒砌而成，宽近九米，高六米多，石块错落有致，对接工整；二层原为菩萨庙，"四清"时期被拆掉，20世纪70年代后期垒建了面向村里的瓦房，瓦房用红石垒墙，青瓦覆顶，厦檐由两根木柱挺起。图为从绿水池村内东西主街之一的南股道东望阁门的景象。

Pavilion gate

The pavilion gate is located east of Lvshuichi Village. The doorway at the lower part of the pavilion gate has a drainage channel for rain water that extends into the village street, built with bluestone, nearly 9 meters wide and more than 6 meters deep. Stones blocks are scattered and neatly connected. In the late 1970s, tiled houses facing the village were built. The tiled houses were built with red stone walls and blue tiles on top. The eaves of the building are raised by two wooden pillars. The picture depicts the eastern view of the pavilion from the perspective of Nangu Road.

民居（一）

　　绿水池村古民居基本是用红石垒砌墙体，选用的石块较为规整，历经岁月洗礼，变成了沧桑的红而泛白的颜色，显得古朴厚重。房顶起脊，黛瓦覆顶，门垛、窗户周边和山脊处用青砖和石灰精心垒砌，像是为红石墙镶上了蓝边，古朴而雅致。

Houses (1)

The ancient houses in Lvshuichi Village are largely built with red stones. The selected stones are typically more regular. After undergoing erosion for many years, they have turned into red and white colors, simply and heavy. Their roofs are ridged, covered with tiles, and the doorposts, the windows, and the eaves are made of blue brick lime.

民居（二）

图为绿水池村后街东北岔道口附近古民居。该民居依山就势建起，街巷随山势弯转，拐角处墙体下部里凹则是为了方便人畜尤其是驴驮通行。建造者不求外形工整，但注重实用。

Houses (2)

This picture depicts the residential area near the Northeast Road fork in Lvshuichi Village. The houses are built in accordance with their placement on the mountain. Streets and lanes twist alongside the mountain, and the lower part of the corner wall is concave to enable the passage of people, animals, and especially donkeys. The builders do not aim for orderly appearance, but rather, focus on the practicality of the design.

民居（三）

　　图为绿水池村近年修建的民居。其主要变化是屋顶不再铺盖青瓦，而是用石板覆顶，这与当地砖瓦窑的消失有关。为了便于三轮车和小汽车通行，街道的石板路也被水泥路代替。

Houses (3)
This picture shows newer houses in Lvshuichi Village. The main difference is that the roof is no longer covered with blue tiles, but with slate panels, which is a direct effect of the disappearance of the local brick kiln. Slate roads have been replaced with cement roads, in order to facilitate the passage of tricycles and cars.

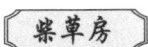

因为地处深山，土地金贵，近年来绿水池人在路边建了些平顶的石头墙小房子，用于存放柴草。

Firewood house

Because Lvshuichi is in a remote mountainous region, land space is precious. In recent years, the Lvshuichi people have built small flat-topped stone-walled storage sheds on the roadside for stacking firewood.

影壁和门楼

在绿水池村，如民居大门面向沟塘或道路，村民一般在门前建筑影壁。绿水池街北侧大部分民居开正阳（南）门，并建有重檐覆瓦的门楼。门楼墙体用青砖垒砌。门楣彩绘戏曲人物、山水柳亭。雀替雕刻祥云龙凤、牡丹连枝。门楣上有一对或两对微微翘起的木制户对。门楼两侧的山墙上也有一对户对，用青石雕刻而成，形似象鼻，托住悬于红石墙上的门楼。

Residential shadow wall and gatehouse

In Lvshuichi Village, if the front of a dwelling is facing a ditch or road, shadow walls are usually built in front of the doorway. Most residences on the north side of Lvshuichi Village open facing zhengyang (south), and are built with double eaves a tiled gatehouse. The doors are built of blue brick. The lintel is generally painted with opera characters, mountain landscapes, and willowed pavilion. Carvings of birds, auspicious clouds, dragons, phoenixes, and peony twigs can also be found. One can also find one or two pairs of small, wooden doors on the lintel.

屋顶和石墙

房顶起脊，黛瓦覆顶，片片青瓦呈现精致韵味，大块红石垒砌的墙体颇具拙朴之风。川人后代和北方人共居一村500多年，形成了南北融合独具特色的民居。此图为绿水池村民居屋顶和石墙。

The roof and the walls of houses

When looking at a traditional roof, its ridges, and delicate black and blue tiles,form quite a charming visual effect. Large red stone walls present a rather simple style. Descendants of the Sichuan people lived together in the village for over 500 years with northerners, forming a unique residential style that integrates both northern and southern aesthetics. This is a typical view of a Lvshuichi house.

> 门　洞

　　图为位于绿水池主街南股道的清代门洞，宽 3 米，高 2.5 米，为青砖石灰垒砌而成，据传已有 200 多年的历史。门洞右侧的院落建于清嘉庆年间，建筑质量比左侧院落高，房外墙上还有元宝形状的拴马石，显示了主人的富裕程度。

The doorway

This picture shows a Qing Dynasty-era archway. It is 3 meters wide and 2.5 meters high, located in the south section of Lvshuichi's main street. It is made of blue brick and limestone. It has a history spanning back over 200 years. The courtyard right of the doorway was built during the Jiaqing Period of the Qing Dynasty. It is of higher quality than the left courtyard. There is a stone for tying up one's horse on the outside wall of the house, which reveals the affluence of the owner.

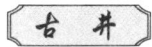

　　图为绿水池村东西主街南股道的古井。古井约有 500 多年的历史，位于进村后小广场的西北角一户古老的民居前。井口石壁光滑，井上可以转动的辘轳和光溜溜的井绳显然仍在为绿水池人汲水使用。

Ancient well

This picture illustrates the ancient well in the south section of the East-West Main Street of Lvshuichi Village. The ancient well has a history of more than 500 years. It is located in the northwest corner of the small square seen directly after entering the village, in front of an ancient folk house. The stone walls at the top of the well are smooth, and the pulley and rope still turn, apparently still being used to draw up water for the people of Lvshuichi.

峡沟水库

图为位于绿水池村附近的约百米深的峡沟水库。沟谷险峻，重岩叠嶂，有"十里峡沟不见天"之说。该水库始建于1958年4月，完全依靠乡土木匠土法测量、计算、设计、修建，1961年8月竣工。1963年，库区连续降雨8天8夜，山洪高出坝顶近两米，水库安然无恙。周恩来总理曾称之为"自力更生，艰苦奋斗的一面旗帜"。

Gorge Reservoir

This picture shows the 100-meters-deep Gorge Reservoir, near Lvshuichi Village. The surrounding valleys are steep and the mountains are encrusted with heavy rock. There is a saying that "The 10-mile gorge blots out the sky". Construction on the reservoir began in April of 1958. Construction completely relied on local carpenters for methods of soil measurement, calculation, design, and construction finished in August of 1961. In 1963, the reservoir area experienced eight days and eight nights of continuous rainfall. Floodwater exceeded the dam crest by nearly two meters, but the reservoir remained safe and sound.

三王村

Sanwang Village

三王村地处太行山丘陵区，村南、北、西三面岭岗环绕，一条季节性河流紧邻村北。全村有居民3000余人，耕地3400亩，属沙河市新城镇管辖。

　　三王村的来历与元顺帝的叔叔潞王曰璟有关。元朝末年，元顺帝丢失天下仓皇北逃。潞王曰璟为保证子嗣安全，将"曰"改为"申"，意为上通天、下通地、中间有田地，并把一口铁锅和一口铜锅摔成18片，交给每个儿子一片，命他们携带逃命，约定日后以锅片相认。曰璟辗转来到此地定居，因其排行第三，就把定居地称为三王村。

　　三王村古民居是典型的冀南太行山丘陵地带四合院建筑。民居墙体底部均为不太规整的青石。普通人家的墙体用土坯干垒，石灰泥抹墙，最后用青砖立表；富裕人家则是里外青砖卧砌到顶，外墙镶嵌青石雕琢而成的元宝状拴马石。墙体都有半米来厚，室内冬暖夏凉。

　　民居屋顶起脊，用三角形木架和木檩、木椽子支撑，上铺青瓦，片片叠压，飞檐翘角。大户人家门楣彩绘吉祥花卉；门楼墀头砖雕各式精美图案，由上中下三部分构成，上部是弧形戗沿砖，中间炉口雕刻牡丹、莲花或武松打虎等图案，下部雕刻简洁的机凳腿图案。民居门窗基本在顶部铺设过木，呈直方形；也有的在顶部青砖裹圈，呈上圆下方形。

　　抗日战争时期，三王村曾经遭遇战火洗礼，至今民居墙壁上还遗留有累累弹痕。

Sanwang Village is located in the hilly area of the Taihang Mountains, surrounded by hills on three sides. A seasonal river is close to the north of the village. There are more than 3,000 residents and 3,400 mu of arable land. It falls under the jurisdiction of Xincheng Town, Shahe City.

The origin of Sanwang Village is related to Emperor Yuan Shun's uncle, Lu Wang Yuejing. In the last years of the Yuan Dynasty, Emperor Yuan Shun lost his grip on the world and fled in panic. In order to ensure the safety of their offsprings, Lu Wang Yuejing changed the character "Yue" in his name to "Shen", which means to go all over the sky, to pass through the earth, and then broke an iron and copper pot into 18 pieces, giving each son a piece. They could then flee their separate ways, using the pot fragments as proof of their mutual recognition. When he came to settle here, because he ranked third, Yuejing called the settlement Sanwang Village.

The representative ancient residence of Sanwang Village is a typical quadrangle building found in the Taihang Mountains' hilly area in southern Hebei Province. The upper part of the walls of these folk houses tends to be built of limestone bricks, and the lower part tends to be composed of irregular bluestones. The upper and outside parts of the walls of rich families is built of blue bricks, with the outside section inlaid with blue stones carved into treasure-resembling shapes. The upper part of the walls of ordinary houses is made of bricks. Inside is a dry barrier of adobe and the lime-mud plaster. These walls are generally half a meter thick, keeping the room warm in winter and cool in summer.

These household rooftops are supported by triangular wooden frames, purlin and rafters. Blue, laminated tiles are on the top, along with ridges and eaves. There are three parts of the gatehouse: the upper part, which curves along the brick, the middle recess, carved with complex patterns like peony, lotus or Wusong figures fighting tigers, which are aimed at expressing certain life expectations, while the lower part is carved with simple patterns of bench legs. The upper and lower floors of the houses are covered with blue bricks, laid over woodwork, most of which are the blocks found on top of door and window frames. A few houses built have brick-carved walls.

During the War of Resistance against Japan, Sanwang Village was often tested by the flames of war.

民居（一）

　　三王村民居的门窗少数为青砖裹圈的拱圈形状，更多的是在顶部铺设过木的方直形状。门口台阶不高，以三到五级为主。过去，人们聚族而居，院院相通。1949年以后，大户人家的房子分给了平民百姓，同住一院的人家不一定是同一家族，因此不少院落之间的通道被堵住。

Houses (1)

The doors and windows of houses in Sanwang Village feature blue bricks wrapped around arch circles. Most of them are block-shaped and overlaid with wood. Doorway steps do not go up that high, mainly staying between three to five levels. In the past, people often gathered together and courtyards were all connected.

民居（二）

图为三王村一所临街的普通民居。民居墙体由石块和青砖垒砌，临街墙上开设方形小窗通风透光。门口横梁之下铺设牙板，山墙炉口阳雕莲花。屋顶起脊，铺设瓦片，脊瓦呈覆筒状，以预防雨水渗漏。

Houses (2)

This picture shows an ordinary folk house facing the street in Sanwang Village. The walls of the dwelling are built of stone brick, and a small square window is opened toward the street in order to facilitate indoor ventilation and light transmission.

民居（三）

　　图为三王村连排的民居。民居墙体下部有少量青石，上部为青砖、白石灰垒砌，古色古香。连排的民居普遍开有侧门，并开有侧面窗户，窗户较小，有上圆下方形，也有方直形状。

Houses (3)

This picture features the adjacent view of a typical Sanwang Village residence. There is a small amount of bluestone in the lower part of the wall, and the upper part is made of brick and white limestone, creating an extraordinarily quaint effect. In general, folk houses generally have side gates, with small side and rear windows. Windows generally have rounded upper sections and squared lower ones, though purely squared windows do exist.

院落（一）

图为三王村的楼房院落。三王村的民居大多坐北朝南，为更好地通风和采光，院落东西窄、南北长。大部分主房是石砖木结构楼房，一般上下层都是五间，一层门窗是方直形状，二层窗户是上圆下方形状。东西厢房是石砖木结构的平顶房，五到七间不等，门窗都是方直形状。院落中通常栽种椿树。

Interior of main residential courtyard (1)

This picture reveals the interior of a main residential courtyard of Sanwang. This is situated in the north facing the south, to allow for better ventilation and lighting. It is narrow in shape, spanning from east to west. The main house is a brick-and-wood structure. Generally speaking, there are five rooms on both the upper and lower floors. Windows on the first floor tend to be squared, while on the second floor they tend to be arched.

院落（二）

　　图为三王村普通人家的平房院落。墙体多用石头垒砌，只有窗户以上用青砖、石灰垒砌；院落较小，石板铺地，院中放置生活必需品。

Interior of main residential courtyard (2)

This picture depicts the courtyard of ordinary people. There are many stones used in the walls of these houses. Only the walls above the windows are laid with blue bricks and lime. The courtyard is small, with slate paving over the ground, on which villagers place their daily necessities.

院落（三）

　　图为三王村一户深宅大院的头进院落。头进院落狭长，厢房门窗对称。头进院落和内院之间是高耸的门楼。内院是封闭性很强的四合院。

Interior of main residential courtyard (3)
The picture depicts the main entrance of a courtyard in Sanwang Village. This entrance is long and narrow, featuring symmetrical doors and windows. The high-rise gatehouse is between the main entrance and inner courtyard. The inner courtyard is a closed quadrangle.

院落（四）

主房每层三间、东西厢房各五间的院落称为"三裹五"院落。图为三王村一处"三裹五"院落的内宅。

Interior of main residential courtyard (4)

The type of courtyard with three main rooms on each floor and five rooms in both east and west sections is called the "Three-Wrap-Five" courtyard. What the picture here depicts is an inner house of this type of courtyard.

门楼

图中民居的门楼起脊飞檐，布瓦顶，脊瓦雕刻牡丹、莲花等吉祥花卉图案；门口木挂落彩绘如意云纹和戏曲场景，色彩艳丽；两侧山墙上部的炉口用青砖雕刻饱满硕大的牡丹花。此图为三王村的一所民居，该民居在1945~1949年曾经为沙河县政府办公场所。

Gatehouse

The doorway of the gatehouse has ridged eaves, roof tiles, carvings of peony, lotus flower and other auspicious flower patterns. At the entrance, the wood is decorated with colorful painted moires and an opera scene of educational significance. This picture shows a folk house in Sanwang Village. The residence was once the office of the Shahe County Government from 1945 to1949.

门楼炉口砖雕

三王村居民习惯在门楼山墙的炉口雕刻武松打虎、牡丹花开、荷花莲蓬等图案，一般用阳刻技法。图中的炉口砖雕用方形青砖雕刻着牡丹花和竹节，花朵硕大饱满，竹节修长直立，寓意富贵而有气节。

The head wall engraving of the gatehouse

Residents of Sanwang Village are accustomed to carving patterns of Wusong figures fighting tigers, peony blossoming, lotus flowers and so on at the entrance to their gatehouses. People generally use engraving techniques. In this picture, the carved peony flowers are made out of square blue bricks. The flowers are large and full, and the bamboo is slender and erect, implying wealth and integrity.

[药王庙]

图为俯瞰三王村药王庙的景象,图中最前面的建筑为药王庙。药王庙曾经是三王村最早的建筑之一,现存药王庙是改革开放后复建的。庙宇红墙黛瓦,庙内保存有三块修庙古石碑。药王庙附近古民居既有青砖青瓦的两层楼,也有青砖墙体水泥顶的平房,院落内高大的梧桐和椿树生机盎然。

Yaowang Temple

This picture offers a view overlooking Yaowang Temple in Sanwang Village. The front building in the picture is Yaowang Temple. Yaowang Temple was once one of the oldest buildings in Sanwang. The currently existing Yaowang Temple was rebuilt after Reform and Opening Up. It is composed of red walls and blue-black tiles. Three ancient monuments are stored in the temple.

神头村

Shentou Village

神头村地处太行浅山区，位于历史文化名山太子岩东麓，距内丘县城西偏北 21 千米，属内丘县南赛乡管辖。该村现有 450 余户人家，1600 多人，村落南、北、西三面环山，龙腾河在村中奔流东去。

神头村村名的来历和春秋时期的神医扁鹊有关。当地民间传说：晋国大夫赵简子生重病不省人事，经扁鹊治愈，便赐给扁鹊 4 万亩蓬山一带的土地。此后扁鹊便栖居于此，上山采药，入乡行医。多年后，扁鹊到了秦国，遭到秦国的太医令李醯嫉妒而被暗杀，噩耗传到蓬山，扁鹊大徒弟虢国太子带人连夜赶到咸阳，将扁鹊的头颅偷回，并用珍贵木材雕刻了身体，一同埋葬在蓬山脚下，并在龙腾河的北侧修建扁鹊庙祭祀。此后，位于龙腾河南北两岸的焦子村和郎家庄合二为一，改名为"神头"村。

住家与茶棚完美结合是神头村民居的特色。茶棚即临时性客栈。每年农历二月二到三月初一庙会期间，为接待来自四面八方的香客，村民们将自家住房设置为供应茶水和临时歇脚的场所——茶棚。茶棚房屋多为平房，一户茶棚一般是两进三套四合院，前一进四合院旁边又连着一个四合院，两个并排的四合院中间是灶台与土炕连接的灶火间，各院落房间小而门多。这种院落结构方便了香客食宿。

庙会期间，香客们上山进香，并进行商品交易，在山上还能看到当地传统的民间表演。

Shentou Village is located in the lower mountain region of Taihang, at the eastern foot of Taiziyan, a famous historical and cultural mountain, and 21 kilometers northwest of the Neiqiu County. Shentou Village falls under the administrative governance of Nansai Township Neiqiu County. The village has a population of more than 450 households and more than 1600 residents. The village is surrounded by mountains on its northern, southern and western sides. The Longteng River runs eastward through the village, with lush trees on the hills and vibrant ecological diversity.

The origin of the village name is related to magic doctor Bian Que, who lived in the Spring and Autumn Period. According to local folklore, a senior official of the Jin State named Zhao Jianzi was seriously ill and unconscious, Bian Que cured him and in return was rewarded 40 thousand mu of land in the area of Pengshan. Bian Que then moved to the newly awarded land, collecting wild herbal remedies in the mountains and practicing medicine in the countryside. Years later, Bian Que arrived at the State of Qin, but was assassinated by an imperial doctor named Li Xi who was envious of his skill. When the grievous news spread back to Pengshan, people felt devastated. His great apprentice, the crown prince of Guo, arrived in Xianyang overnight, stole back his head and made a carving of his body out of wood. They buried this body at the foot of Pengshan Mountain, also building a sacrificial temple north of Longteng River. After this, Jiaozi Village and Lang Village on both sides of the river became one united village and adopted a new name, "Shentou".

What makes Shentaou dwellings unique is the seamless way with which they integrate household courtyards with their tea houses. The tea house functions as a temporary inn. During the temple fair from February 2nd to March 1st of the lunar calendar, pilgrims from all directions come and go in constant streams. To accommodate them, tea houses in villages along the way and in Shentou Village are set up. Tea houses tend to be larger than single-story residential bungalows. One tea house can be connected to two or three quadrangle courtyards. These courtyards each have many small rooms and many connecting doors. In the middle of the courtyards is often a communal stove and heatable adobe kang, useful for guests lodging nearby.

At the temple fair in Shentou Village, people can see traditional local folk performances. During the temple fair, pilgrims can ascend the mountain single-file and offer incense to the Buddha as well as trade with others.

民居 （一）

神头村的民居多以石块和石灰垒砌，平房居多，整体风格比较古朴。门楼较为低矮，少有精雕细刻。大部分院落较小，多是四合院，房间小而多，能够为每年二三月庙会期间到来的四方信众提供住宿。图为一所普通民居。

Exterior view of ordinary residential building (1)

Shentou ancient houses are built with stones and limestone base, and most are simple bungalows. The gatehouses are relatively low and seldom carved with details. Most courtyards are small and quadrangle with many small rooms, which can provide accommodations for the believers of all stripes who visit for the annual temple fair in February and March. What is drawn in this picture is an ordinary folk house.

民居（二）

　　神头村有不少前后相连、左右相通的连体院落。一般情况下，院主人住在里院上房，外院是分成若干个房间的四合院，用于招待宾客。此图为某户人家的主人所居住的上房。

Exterior view of ordinary residential building (2)
There are many contiguous courtyards in Shentou Village. Generally, the owner of the house lives in one of the main rooms of the inner courtyard, and the outer courtyard is a quadrangle divided into several rooms, which are used to entertain guests. This picture features one of the main rooms where an owner might live.

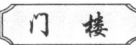

　　图为神头村某巷子里一户人家的门楼。该门楼的门楣正中央刻写一个"安"字，木挂落、木垂柱保存完好，门墩为天然木材所制，门前有三级较低矮的青石台阶。

Gatehouse

This picture shows the gatehouse of a family's house in an alleyway, as well as the house's shed in front of the doorway. The middle of the lintel of the gatehouse was engraved with the Chinese character "an", intricate fascia carvings, and wooden columns are all preserved well. The gate blocks are made of natural lumber. Three steps made of bluestone are in front of the door.

| 厦 棚 |

　　图为神头村某街巷拐角处的一个厦棚。由于住户的门口正好开在巷子拐角处，于是户主利用左右两侧墙体，在门口前搭建了一个厦棚，既方便行人避雨，还可以在墙角处存放些杂物。

The shed
This picture shows a shed on the corner of one of Shentou Village's streets. The door in the corner of the alleyway is opened, showing that both sides of the wall are in use. A shed has been built in front of the door, not only to offer shelter to guests and passersby, but also as a place of storage for various items.

扁鹊庙（一）

图为神头村扁鹊庙全景。据《魏书·地形志》记载，扁鹊庙至少有1500多年的历史，现存为元代建筑。扁鹊庙建有扁鹊殿、药王殿、玉皇殿、三清殿等道教建筑，总占地面积约3.72万平方米。

The panorama of Bian Que Temple (1)

This picture is a panorama of the Bian Que Temple. According to records found in "Wei Shu Topography", Bian Que Temple has at least 1,500 years of history, and the currently existing building was built during the Yuan Dynasty. The temple holds Taoist architecture, such as the Hall of Bian Que, the Palace of the Medicine King, the Hall of the Jade Emperor, and the Hall of Sanqing, covering a total area of roughly 37.2 thousand square meters.

扁鹊庙（二）

图为神头村扁鹊庙山门。该门于 1999 年 8 月修复完成，坐落于 12 级石台阶之上，拱顶飞檐，明柱挺立，宽门大窗，彩绘木枋。门前蹲坐一对威武的石狮子。

The panorama of Bian Que Temple (2)

This picture features the Mountain Gate of Bian Que Temple in Shentou Village. The gate was restored and completed in August of 1999. It is located on 12 stone steps, with vaulted eaves, upright columns, wide doors, painted wooden beams and large windows. A pair of mighty stone lions rests in front of the entrance.

扁鹊庙（三）

图为神头村扁鹊庙前山岩上的九龙柏。柏树是人们为怀念具有高尚医德和高超医术的名医扁鹊所植，已有千余年历史。树根似龙爪，紧紧抓住块块岩石，树干遒劲盘旋，枝叶繁茂。

The panorama of Bian Que Temple (3)

This picture shows the Nine-dragon Cypress on the rock in front of Bian Que Temple in Shentou. Cypress trees are planted in remembrance of the noble Bian Que, renowned doctor of the land. Its history spans over a thousand years. The roots of the tree are like the claws of a dragon, grasping the rocks tightly. The trunk twists vigorously, beneath flourishing branches and leaves.

> 神头庙会

神头村的庙会因祭祀扁鹊而形成，历史悠久，一年数次，其中三月初一规模最大。据明朝成化二十三年（1488年）《重修扁鹊山庙记》碑载，庙会涉及顺德府、保定府、广平府三府18县。庙会期间，人山人海，车水马龙，民间艺术表演丰富多彩。

The Shentou Temple Fair

The Shentou Temple Fair was formed in honour of Bian Que, with a long history of being held several times a year. The fair is most robust in March. According to the inscription on the "Repairs of Bian Que Mountain Temple" dating back to the 23rd year of Chenghua in the Ming Dynasty (1488), the fair has involved the Shunde, Baoding and Guangping Prefecture, spanning 18 counties. During the fair, there is a sea of people, thronging foot traffic, and colorful folk art performances.

黄岔村
Huangcha Village

黄岔村位于邢台市西北太行深山区，地处凌霄山北侧河岔交汇地带，属内丘县獐獏乡管辖。黄岔村现有65户、240多人，山场近万亩。相传黄岔原名黄卡，曾是东汉末年黄巾军设立哨卡之地，后黄卡逐渐演变为黄岔。

　　黄岔村是一个典型的冀南太行石灰岩山区小村庄，民居院落保存基本完好。村内石头房屋依山随形，高低错落，有的石头房直接用天然山石作为墙壁，有的民居排水沟就凿刻在门口旁天然大石块上。黄岔民居大多为单层建筑，少数为二层楼房。院落有单体式、连体式、四合院式，偶有二进院落。墙体建筑材料均为就地取材的青石，屋顶以平檐、石灰砂石顶为主。

　　黄岔村历史文化厚重。这里是泜水南支源头，即《山海经》所谓"敦与山，泜水出其阴"所在地。东汉末年，凌霄山是黄巾起义军领袖张角的中央大寨所在地，山上现今仍遗存有黄巾军中央大寨石头寨墙。遗址约5000米长，寨墙宽度1~1.5米，高达4~5米。遗址区布满黄巾军营房残垣断壁，有执行军法的水牢，还有一些石臼等生活用具遗迹。

　　黄岔村还曾是抗日根据地堡垒村。抗日战争时期，这里是沟通冀南和太行抗日根据地的重要交通站。

Huangcha Village is located in deep the Taihang mountain area northwest of Xingtai City and on the north side of the historical and cultural Lingxiao Mountain, which is also an intersection of rivers. It falls under the jurisdiction of Zhangmo Township in Neiqiu County. Currently, there are 65 households in Huangcha Village, totaling over 240 residents. Hilly fields nearby account for roughly 10,000 mu of land. According to legend, Huangcha's original name was Huangqia, and later gradually evolved into Huangcha.

Huangcha is a typical small village found throughout the Taihang limestone mountain area of Hebei Province. These ancient villages are basically still intact. Stone residential homes in the village follow the contour of mountains, and different houses have varying heights. Some of them use a rock slab as the back wall, while some drainage passageways are carved into natural rock formations. Most of the houses in Huangcha are single-story buildings. Several have two stories. Courtyards tend to adopt single interconnected style orienting around quadrangle courtyard design, though occasionally adopting two-way layouts. The walls are largely made of locally obtained blue stone. In addition, most rooftops feature flat limestone eaves.

Huangcha Village has a long and rich history.

At the conclusion of the Eastern Han Dynasty, Lingxiao Mountain was the central fortress of the Yellow Turban Army, whose leader Zhang Jiao was stationed therein. One can still see a five-kilometer-long gated wall on the mountain to this day. The wall is approximately 1 to 1.5 meters wide and 4 to 5 meters high. The surrounding ruins contain the remnants of their barracks, water prisons used for punishment under military law, and stone mortars, which were likely used by the rebels for grinding rice noodles.

Huangcha Village was also a staging area for anti-Japan war efforts. During the War of Resistance against Japan, Huangcha functioned as a strong fortress of resistance for the rebels fighting against the Japanese.

图为黄岔村的雪景。白雪覆盖大地、屋顶,树枝裹满雪花,村落更加宁静。图中石桥附近的石头房曾经是抗日战争时期冀西游击总队内丘独立营的营部。

Huangcha in snow

This picture shows Huangcha's snow-covered landscape. Snow covers the ground and rooftops, and the tree branches are covered with snowflakes. This lets the village become more peaceful. In this picture, the stone house near the stone bridge used to be the camp headquarters of the Independent Hill Battalion of the guerrilla army of western Hebei during the War of Resistance against Japan.

民居（一）

　　因黄岔村地处山沟，民居呈阶梯坐落，院落较狭小，村民习惯在院落附近搭建柴草棚、羊圈和厕所，在其间的零星地块见缝插针地栽种树木，种植瓜菜。

Houses (1)
Because Huangcha Village is located in a valley, its residential dwellings have staircases, and their courtyards are narrow. Villagers are accustomed to building near their courtyard firewood sheds, sheep pens and toilets, alongside scattered plots of trees, melons and vegetables.

民居（二）

黄岔村民居受地形地势影响，房屋高低走向不一致，以背风向阳、有利生产生活为建筑原则。

Houses (2)

Affected by the topography and terrain, the distribution of Huangcha's houses is irregular, and the tendencies of higher and lower houses are not consistent. In general, homes tend to abide by the principle of having the lee side facing the sun, which is beneficial for production.

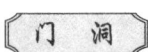

图为黄岔村一户人家的门洞。木制大门随意敞开，散养的柴鸡在门口走来走去，门洞里放着铁锨等劳动工具，这是黄岔随处可见的景象。

Doorways of ordinary families

This picture is a doorway of an ordinary family in Huangcha Village. The chai chickens are walking to and fro at the opened wooden doorway. Shovels and other tools of labor are placed beside the doorway. This is a scene that can be seen everywhere in Huangcha.

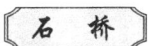

图为黄岔村的石桥。这里原有一座古老的木桥，1963年大洪水时木桥被冲毁，其后才建起了石桥。桥下的溪流发源于凌霄山北坡，是泜河的南支流。

Stone bridge

There used to be an ancient wooden bridge here that was destroyed by flood in 1963. Later, Huangcha's villagers built a stone bridge in its place. The valley stream under the bridge originates from the northern slope of Lingxiao Mountain and is the southern branch of the Zhi River.

石台阶和石碾子

  黄岔村民居的石台阶比较宽大,石碾盘也很厚重,石磙两侧的雕花不相同。这些都是用当地出产的青石雕琢而成的。

The stone steps and stone mill

The stone steps of Huangcha residences are very wide and the stone grinding base is also very large and thick. The carvings on both sides of the stone mill are different. They are all carved with locally produced blue stone.

汉阙（一）

图为村民在黄岔村南、凌霄山北坡所建的仿汉代建筑——汉阙。黄岔原名黄卡，东汉末年是凌霄山上黄巾军中央大寨的哨所。今人在村头建造象征着哨所的汉阙以纪念黄岔村的这段历史。

Han Palace (1)

This picture depicts the imitation Han Dynasty building called Han Palace, which was built by Han descendants. Huangcha's original name is Huangqia. It was the former sentry post in charge of guarding the Yellow Turban Army's central stockade village on Lingxiao Mountain. Today, in memory of this history, people at the head of the village have built a symbol of the the outpost.

汉阙（二）

图为黄岔村汉阙内的景象。墙壁上粘贴当地出产的石砖，木制楼梯直通顶部瞭望楼。

Han Palace (2)

This picture shows the scene inside Han Palace. The walls are covered with locally produced stone bricks and wooden staircases lead to the top of the building.

后 记

终于要出版了。早在去年，我们就开始着手这本书的绘画和撰写工作。中间，作为这本书的作者，我们多次和出版社的编辑进行沟通、交流，也根据出版社的意见，对画稿和文稿进行了多次补充和修改。

始于书，而不限于书，也不仅仅止于书。这一切，因为古村落而结缘。

我们对古村落的关注和大量采写，一方面是因为工作，另一方面却完全是因为热爱，或者是对古村落保护、发展的一份责任。

我们曾经成立过一个专门的采访团，规模不大，但是这个采访团里涉及多个行业的专家，有古村落立档调查的管理者，有古村落研究专家，有摄影家，有画家，有记者；能够加入这个采访团的，无一不是关注和热爱古村落的人。

我们跋山涉水，邢台市太行山区的数十个古村落都留下了我们的足迹。为了探访古村落，我们的画家在山里一待就是几个月；为了探访古村落，我们翻过了邢台市能说上名字和说不上名字的大小山川；为了探访古村落，我们在采写的旅途中曾遭遇事故惊险——轮胎爆胎，紧挨车的一侧就是悬崖；为了探访古村落，我们差点被山洪堵在山里。

有汗水，也有很多的快乐和惊喜：村里做的大锅菜是真心好吃；采一束山间雏菊带回家，霎时整个房间都充满了田野的清香；山间路上，偶尔也能遇到野兔、野鸡之类的小动物从身边飞快地跑过……然而，对我们来说最大的快乐，还是发现一处保存完好、建筑有特点的古村落，当然还有和许许多多淳朴的乡亲成了老熟人、好朋友。

一切，都源于对古村落的热爱。

这本书能出来，我们要感谢的人有很多。感谢学苑出版社领导和编辑的支持，没有他们对中国传统文化的情怀，就不会有这本书的出版。而在出版过程中，我们也确实领略到了出版社编辑所特有的严谨和认真精神。感谢邢台市委宣传部、邢台市文联、邢台市民协领导对这本书的支持和关爱。在书的绘画、撰写过程中，他们多次询问、协调编绘的进度问题，并及时解决相关难题。感谢市政府研究室冀胜利主任、王喜恩调研员等给予的无私支持。感谢乡镇里那么多古村落热心人士，如邢台县路罗镇镇长王立斌，他对这本书的编写给予了很多支持。路罗镇是个邢台古村落集群所在地，当地政府从上到下，一直很重视古村落的保护和开发。如鱼林沟的李修林、胡海书，提供了很多文字资料。如当时路罗镇政府的工作人员李霞，她不辞辛苦、任劳任怨地给我们做向导。还有时任内丘县獐獏乡党委书记戎文革、沙河市新城镇党委书记乔万国，都给我们这本书的绘画、撰写工作提供了大量帮助。

感谢那么多一直从事古村落保护和研究工作的学者、专家、摄影家、画家、媒体人以及古村落爱好者们，没有他们的努力和贡献，我们这本书会缺少很多分量。如冀彤军、李恒坤、文天平、王云、李自歧、戴杰、张平勤、张子乾、李永胜、许向丁，等等。还要感谢沙河市王硇村支书王现增、邢台县英谈村支书张书明、内丘县黄岔村支书刘志国这些热心和开明人士。

历史遗存面临的残酷在于，一旦毁灭，永不可真实复原。随着岁月的流逝，很多古村落正在消失，或者风貌不再。保护好这些古村落，是保护一段历史，保护一种文化，保护一种生活，也是在小心地呵护一段记忆、一种情怀。

在保护古村落这条路上，我们会继续前行。

张军昱

2018年10月25日

Postscript

At last it's published. As early as last year, we began painting and compiling this book. Throughout the process, as the authors of this book, we entered into frequent communication and interaction with the editors of the publishing house. As a result of this cooperative spirit, we supplemented and revised the drawings and manuscripts many times in accordance with the opinions of the publishing house.

It all started with a book. But, however, it was not limited to a book, nor was it held back by one. All of this is because of the ancient villages—because of them, we became attached to the project.

We gave these ancient villages our utmost care and attention, partly because of work, partly because of love, and partly because of a cultural duty to research and protect their development.

We established a special group for conducting interviews. It was not large in scope, but the team featured a manager in charge of establishing the survey, experts on ancient villages, photographers, painters, journalists, and others heralding from diverse fields. Without exception, all participants held unbridled interest and cared deeply for ancient villages.

We traveled over mountains and rivers, leaving our footprints in dozens of ancient villages of Xingtai City. Our painter stayed in the mountains with the locals for months at a time to produce authentic works; in the course of traveling to remote villages, we crossed innumerable mountains and rivers, some whose names we knew and some we did not; in order to gather materials necessary for completing a section of writing, the tire of our vehicle burst beside a sheer cliff; in another particular episode, we were nearly trapped by a mountain flood.

There was much sweat involved, but also much happiness. We salivated over fresh village delicacies; fragrant daisies abounded the roadside, whose wild scent filled many rooms; and pheasants and other small animals caught our gazes on the mountainsides. However, for us, the greatest happiness was found in the discovery of ancient villages with well-preserved characteristic architecture, as well as becoming good friends with the locals.

It all comes from the love of ancient villages.

There are a lot of people to thank in the production and release of this book.

Thanks to the support of Xueyuan Publishing House. This book could not have been published without their strong feelings for traditional Chinese culture. In the process of publishing, we deeply appreciate the special rigor and seriousness their editors brought to the table. Thanks to the support and care of leaders at the Xingtai Publicity Department, Xingtai Literary Federation and Xingtai Citizen Association. In the process of both painting and writing, their consultation was crucial for coordinating progress and solving issues in a timely manner. Thanks to so many ancient village enthusiasts, such as Wang Libin, Mayor of Luluo, Xingtai County. He provided abundant support for the book. Luluo Town is made up of a cluster of ancient Xingtai villages, and from top to bottom in the local government, he has always attached great importance to the protection and development of ancient villages. For example, Li Xiulin and Hu Haishu of Yulingou provided us with abundant textual materials. Moreover, Li Xia, a staff member of the Luoluo Town Government at that time, offered guidance on many issues, never complaining once. At that time, the Secretary of the Party Committee in Neiqiu County, River Deer Township, Rong Wenge, and the Secretary of the Xincheng Town Party Committee of Shahe City, Qiao Wanguo, all provided ample help in writing and painting this book.

Thanks to the many scholars, experts, photographers, painters, media figures, and ancient village enthusiasts who have been engaged in the conservation and research of ancient villages. Without their efforts and contributions, the quality of our book would surely suffer. For example, Ji Tongjun, Li Hengkun, Wen Tianping, Wang Yun, Li Ziqi, Dai Jie, Zhang Pingqin, Zhang Ziqian, Li Yongsheng, Xu Xiangding, and many others all provided instrumental feedback. We would also like to thank Wang Xianzeng, Secretary of Wangnao Village in Shahe City, Zhang Shuming, Secretary of Yingtan Village Branch of Xingtai County, and Liu Zhiguo, Secretary of Huangcha Village Branch of Neiqiu County, for their enthusiastic and enlightening guidance.

There is a sort of cruelty in the destructive capacity of time: historical remains, once destroyed, can never again be truly restored. In the long river of time, many good ancient villages have disappeared, art styles have transformed beyond recognition or even been forgotten. To protect these ancient villages is to protect a kind of history, a kind of culture and a kind of life. It is also to care for a kind of memory and treasure a kind of sentiment.

On this road, we move onward!

Zhang Junyu
October 25th, 2018